BETWEEN FRAMES

Ted Lowe talking to Frank Butler

Ted Lowe

TALKING TO FRANK BUTLER

Between Frames

ADAM & CHARLES BLACK · LONDON

First published in 1984 by A & C Black (Publishers) Ltd.,
35 Bedford Row, London WC1R 4JH

Designed by Douglas Martin Associates
Set in 10 on 14pt Paladium by Armitage Typo/Graphics Ltd
Printed and bound by Hazell Watson & Viney, Aylesbury, Bucks.

ACKNOWLEDGEMENTS

The authors and publishers would like to thank the following for their co-operation in compiling this book and for kind permission to reproduce photographs:

John Carty *(Cue World)*, Norman Clare (E. & A. Clare),
Bruce Donkin (E. J. Riley), Stephen Gross (Newmarket Moat House),
Nick Hunter (BBC), Jim Latham, Dolly Lindrum (Melbourne, Australia),
Marcus Marsh, David Muscroft, Reg Perrin (BBC),
Trog, Harry Wragg, Queen's Moat Houses PLC, *Lancashire Evening Post*,
News of the World, Northern Counties Newspapers Ltd., Central Press,
the Press Association
and the professional players.

Lowe, Ted
Between frames.
1. Lowe, Ted 2. Snooker players—Biography
I. Title II. Butler, Frank
794.7'35'0924 GV900.S6

ISBN 0-7136-2446-9

Contents

Introduction

BETWEEN FRAMES is the story of a shy country boy, who would probably have stayed that way and joined one of the racing stables around Lambourn where he was born but for his early love of billiards and snooker.

From the age of seven, Ted Lowe was completely dedicated to the game; and it was this dedication that was responsible for his progress from a tatty billiards room in a Lambourn pub to the bright lights of Leicester Square and London's West End, and later led to travels still farther afield to Australia, New Zealand, Singapore, Hong Kong and other distant lands where the game of snooker is cherished.

Ted's soothing Berkshire burr has earned him the title of 'Whispering Ted' and is instantly recognised by millions of television fans in Britain and Australia. His controlled comments are authoritative and unobtrusive; he is a guide to the less knowledgeable fan and is also readily accepted by the expert. During the Championships of the World—the United Kingdom, the Masters, World Team Classic or Pot Black—the voice of Ted Lowe is as distinctive as that of Dan Maskell on tennis or that of John Arlott on cricket.

Ted Lowe is not only Mr Television, he is also Mr Snooker. He is the most experienced executive in the game, and the most knowledgeable, not just as a commentator but as an organiser and adjudicator. A former amateur player who once reached the English amateur snooker championships semi-final, he was a founder member of both the Players Association and the Referees Association, and was already President of the London and Home Counties Billards and Snooker Association and patron of Westerham Snooker League, when elected President of the Billiards and Snooker Control Council, the world governing body, in 1982. As the former manager of the Leicester Square Hall, the intimate home of billiards and snooker known as 'Thurston's' until it was bombed during the last war, Ted Lowe organised the world championships and all the major tournaments for a decade, becoming a friend not only of the great Joe Davis, but of every snooker champion as well as many stars of show business.

Ted Lowe is the Voice of Snooker. Unseen by viewers, Ted has done much to promote the sport and to keep it alive in its darkest years when—before colour television—it looked like going under. His involvement with BBC's Pot Black series in 1969 proved the turning point for the popularity of snooker, transforming a dying sport with only a handful of capable professionals remaining into the biggest booming sport in Britain and the Commonwealth. Now not only has snooker a television audience of millions, but the young snooker stars are fast becoming the new millionaires of sport; they all owe a great deal to Ted Lowe's persistent refusal to accept that snooker was a sport without a spectator audience.

Between Frames is Ted Lowe's story as related to Frank Butler, Fleet Street's longest serving sports editor and national award-winning columnist, who knew all the great champions of sport, and who was honoured with the OBE for his services to sports writing. Here you will find stories of the stars from Joe Davis to Steve Davis and beyond—of the unpredictable Alex 'Hurricane' Higgins, the stylish Ray Reardon, of quiet Terry Griffiths, handsome Tony Knowles and many more. For all snooker fans, men and women, young or old, *Between Frames* will make fascinating reading.

Frank Butler and Ted Lowe.

CHAPTER 1

The Good Old Days

JUST one evening in the autumn of 1945 was to change my life completely, though I was quite unaware of it at the time. This was the occasion of my first meeting with Joe Davis and Horace Lindrum. Joe, of course, was the greatest snooker player I ever watched; Horace was the nephew of Australia's Walter Lindrum, undeniably the finest billiards player the world has known. Although I did not know it then, Joe and Horace were to become life-long friends to me in completely different ways—Joe as the paternal companion, always ready to offer counsel and to help me through my career, Horace as more of a brother or a pal.

But to go back to the beginning. I was born in the racing village of Lambourn in Berkshire, the first child of Ernest Lowe, known as 'Dodger'—he was always dodging from one bar to another—who was travelling head lad with the well-known racing stables of Ossie Bell. My father and I were born under the same roof, in a cottage-type house in Newbury Street. All my father's family seemed to be in racing. My grandfather was a tout for the *Sporting Life* and, though I was only between seven and eight years old at the time, I still recall the excitement when Felstead won the Derby in 1928 and my father proudly led the horse into our tiny village—to the delight of the locals who were all a little richer.

My mother's family had always been connected with public-houses. The Lamb at Lambourn had been in her family for several generations and when I first saw the light of day, the Lamb was run by mother's sister and her husband Jim Staddon. I suppose this fact more than any other brought me into the world of billiards when I was only seven, a twist of fate for which I am forever grateful, for my official education was restricted to the village school and this ended two months before my fourteenth birthday. However, when I was only ten I became, in a sense, an apprentice publican. My daily chores included stocking up shelves, checking the beer, wines and spirits, looking after the cellars, cigarettes, biscuits, crisps and snacks. It was hard and unrewarding work. Only one bonus made it all worthwhile. In the small billiards room was a quarter-size billiards table which was to keep me occupied for hours. During school holidays and at any time when I had a break I would play billiards, always by myself; on looking back, I realise how lonely my childhood was, yet I derived more pleasure, I feel sure, from practising on that little table, than did the sons of rich parents from expensive toys. I was so completely hooked on the thought of becoming a

Ted astride his first bicycle at thirteen, and a few years later astride his first horse—but Ted had no ambition to become a jockey. Already a billiard table appealed more than a racing stable.

Ted's dad Ernest Lowe, nicknamed 'Dodger', with *Impreceptable,* a half-brother to *Denbigh,* at Ossie Bell's Lambourn stable.

Dodger Lowe lines up with Billy Parvin's team of steeple-chasers at his stables at Upavon, Wiltshire.

Lowe Senior parades another 'resident' of Ossie Bell's stable round the paddock.

Felstead, 1928 Derby winner, is led in by Sir Hugo Cunliffe-Owen. The whole of Lambourn celebrated.

During Ted's last months in Lambourn in 1934, *Windsor Lad,* trained by Marcus Marsh, won the Derby—the first of Charlie Smirke's four Derby winners.

billiards champion that I even bought myself a set of marbles so that when I couldn't get to the little room, I could at least practise on the kitchen table. It did not, of course, have pockets but it did enable me to improve my judgement of angles and cannons.

We were a closely-knit family. Several uncles and aunts on my mother's side were frequent visitors to Lambourn and, unbeknown to me, one of my uncles arranged with my father that when I left school I should spend some time helping in their larger pub at Streatham in south-west London to further my apprenticeship, as mother and father clearly assumed that I would follow the family tradition and become a publican. Dad didn't want me to go into racing, knowing I would never make the weight as a jockey.

The work was now much harder because the Pied Bull was a larger pub, but once again there was some consolation for me. I was nearly fourteen and, though unhappy at leaving Lambourn, when I learned that the Pied Bull had a full-size billiards table, my protests slackened off. It was in that room at Streatham that I learned to play snooker for the first time and, whilst I had flirted with billiards for seven years, I now fell madly in love with snooker. The honeymoon is still going on.

I took to potting like a duck to water. Perhaps the right blend was there from birth. My father was a sporting type and my mother belonged to a pub family. Call it beer and skittles if you like, but snooker was to take me into the glamour of London's Leicester Square, Piccadilly and Soho, and into a new world of champagne, caviar and showbiz.

However, the bright life was still a long way off for me. My menial duties at Streatham consisted of lighting fires, cleaning out lavatories and washing up endless glasses. But serving behind the bar gave much-needed confidence to a shy boy. I was not rebellious for the simple reason that every spare minute was spent in the billiards room experimenting on that wonderful full-size table. I became so proficient that customers began to take notice and my uncle promoted me to official marker. I was over the moon and felt a very important young man. Thus inspired, my game began to improve so rapidly that within twelve months I could almost guarantee making a break of between sixty and eighty in any three frames. When the pub had closed I would spend every minute practising with my cousin Tom and if ever at any time a stranger put his head round the door, I would challenge—or perhaps it would be more true to say plead with—him to give me a game. Even as a youngster I realised competition was more important than 'beating myself'.

But there were days when I was desperately lonely. On these occasions I longed to be back in Lambourn. In my village I knew everybody. I could talk to boys of my own age or even to older men, but London was an unfriendly and lonely place for me. My uncle gave me one day off a week. For months I was content to spend it in the billiards room but my uncle and aunt quite rightly thought I should get away occasionally and encouraged me to explore the heart of London, the West End or the City, to broaden my education. I was told to discover all the places that the tourist is advised to visit—Buckingham Palace, the Houses of Parliament, Westminster Abbey, the Tower of London and other monuments of history.

I know they were correct in their thinking but visiting the Tower alone didn't appeal to me. Instead, I inquired of a friendly policeman the best way to get to Thurston's. To me it was a hallowed name. I knew that great billiards champions such as Walter Lindrum, Tom Newman, Willie Smith, Melbourne Inman, Tom Reece and Joe Davis had demonstrated their skill there. What a thrill it was for me to spend the few shillings I had saved from my pub duties to attend afternoon sessions. My biggest thrill was seeing Joe Davis in action. Joe was by now the greatest name in both billiards and snooker. His first choice was snooker and he was able to persuade older players to take part in an exhibition frame of snooker after the more serious billiards matches were over. It was then that Joe came to life. His eyes sparkled as he took up a more bellicose stance and a sharper cue action. He was on the attack and the balls obeyed him! The older men, schooled in the finesse of billiards, played more cautiously and it was obvious they did not take to the new twenty-two ball game. Perhaps it was my youth, but I became excited every time Davis came to the table. He was my hero but I dared not approach him at this stage. I was too shy even to ask the great man for his autograph. Little did I know that in not too many years I was to meet him and become a friend and business associate.

I was at the impressionable age of sixteen when, as I was brushing and ironing the billiards table at Streatham one morning, a cheerful sort of character strolled into the room and asked if I would give him a game of snooker. I jumped at the chance and during the first frame felt I had found a friend. Soon I was telling him of my loneliness. He explained that he was part of a double act on the variety halls known as Pat and Vera Lennox and that I was welcome on my next day off to come to the Kingston Empire, watch the show and come backstage afterwards.

In the days long before television, the variety stars were the biggest entertainers in show business and were a fine bunch of troupers. I had heard of this act, and I followed Pat and Vera Lennox to every one of the Moss Empires throughout London. After twelve months I don't think there was a variety theatre in town I had not visited and where I had not spent time backstage meeting other artistes. They were big names in their day but, alas, are long forgotten now—though one of the immortals I had the honour to shake hands with at the Holborn Empire was Fats Waller. I shall never forget the kindness and friendship of Pat and Vera Lennox. They lived just around the corner from the Pied Bull and I spent most Sunday evenings with them. It was at their home that I met a young man named Teddy Formby. He was the youngest of three Formby brothers—Teddy, Frank and George. George was internationally famous with his ukelele and popular songs. Teddy worked for a theatrical agency in Leicester Square, which meant I had made another friend to call in on during my visits to Thurston's. Teddy's mother, Mrs 'Plum' Formby, took to me and I became a regular visitor to their home in Clapham. Thanks to all these friends I developed from a quiet, lonely lad into a happy teenager thoroughly enjoying my connections with snooker and the stage.

By the time I was eighteen I had built up quite a local reputation as a useful amateur

Ted's early association with the variety stage encouraged him to try a little impersonating. Here *(top right)* Maurice Chevalier is the target. Years later *(below)* hamming it up at a charity 'do' we see the Reverend Ted Lowe, and on another such occasion *(top left)* as a Chelsea Pensioner.

snooker player. As the marker I had the knack of speedily working out how many snookers were required for a player well behind. 'You need three snookers and all the colours and you can win by three', I would say in a flash and because I had my sums correct, my mathematics became a gimmick with the customers.

Regular visitors to the Pied Bull were the Smith family, who owned Smith Meters, a flourishing business manufacturing gas meters for private homes. The men in the family enjoyed a game of snooker and must have been impressed with my quick totting up. They were looking for a bright young man to go into their estimating and rate-fixing department, and they asked me to take the job. I was tired of working six days a week in the pub so I left the Pied Bull and joined Smith Meters for what seemed to me then the princely wages of twenty-seven shillings a week. It caused a family row. My uncle and aunt accused me of being ungrateful, and it was more than two years before they even spoke to me again.

Within a year of joining Smith Meters, Britain and Germany were at war. I would have joined the RAF but I was now working in a reserved occupation at the factory and I remained with them until the end of the war. I was surprised to find that a factory with thousands of employees was without any social activity and was able to persuade the Smiths to let me start up a social club. They allowed me to purchase two Nissen huts and, more important to me, a billiards table. The war had ended by the time it was ready to open in September, 1945, and I wrote to Joe Davis inviting him to play an exhibition game for our opening night. He agreed, and I then read in the press that Horace Lindrum was on a boat bound for England. I wired the ship and received confirmation that he would appear with Joe. It was to be his first appearance in England and the whole of the billiards world wanted to be there. I shall never forget playing one frame against Joe Davis that night—and beating him! I must add that Joe insisted on my receiving six blacks, but I sank the last red and all the colours and the maestro was quietly impressed. The next thing I knew was that John Bissett, then Chairman of the Billiards Association and Control Council, invited me to enter the All-England snooker championship and I reached the semi-final. But more important than this to me was the fact that Mr Eric Taylor, an executive of W. Jelks and Sons, the big manufacturers of tables and accessories, invited me to be interviewed by the boss, Mr Bob Jelks. They were looking for a young man to become general manager of the new Leicester Square Hall which they were opening in 1946 to replace Thurston's, which had been bombed during the war.

I could hardly believe my luck. Thurston's to me was a place to be revered. Also, I had married in 1942 and one month before this opportunity came, my wife and I had been overjoyed by the birth of our daughter Margaret, so I was looking for a better-paid job to support my family. I was over the moon. Here I was at twenty-six with the fancy title of general manager of Leicester Square Hall, with a big salary compared with my low wages at Streatham, and a dinner jacket thrown in!

Being the youngest general manager in the West End was a big step up for the boy who

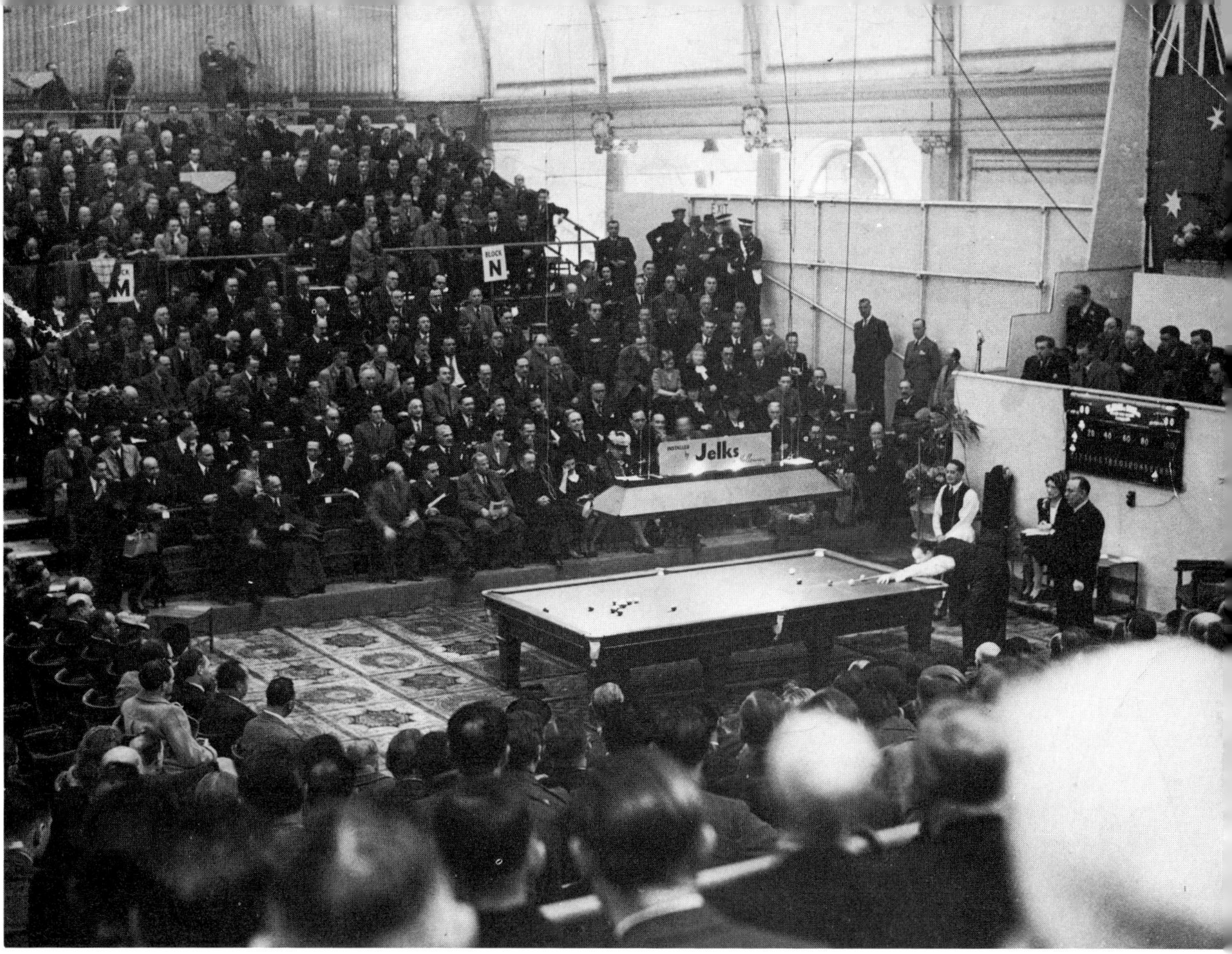

Joe Davis retaining his world championship by beating Horace Lindrum at the Horticultural Hall, Westminster, in 1945. The match saw the largest snooker attendance until the world championships moved to the Crucible Theatre in Sheffield in 1977.

Ted in his early twenties as an amateur who reached the semi-finals of the All-England snooker championships.

The youngest general manager in the West End: Ted in his tiny office at Leicester Square Hall after his appointment in 1947.

Pre-war Thurston's, from a painting in 1938 by Charles Cundall, of a 1932 match between Tom Newman (in action) and Joe Davis (behind him), with Charles Chambers, the famous referee, at the other end of the table.

The outside of Thurston's on the morning after it was shattered by bombing in 1940.

Air raid damage at Thurston's put paid to the famous table on which Walter Lindrum, the world's greatest billiards player, scored his record 4,137 break.

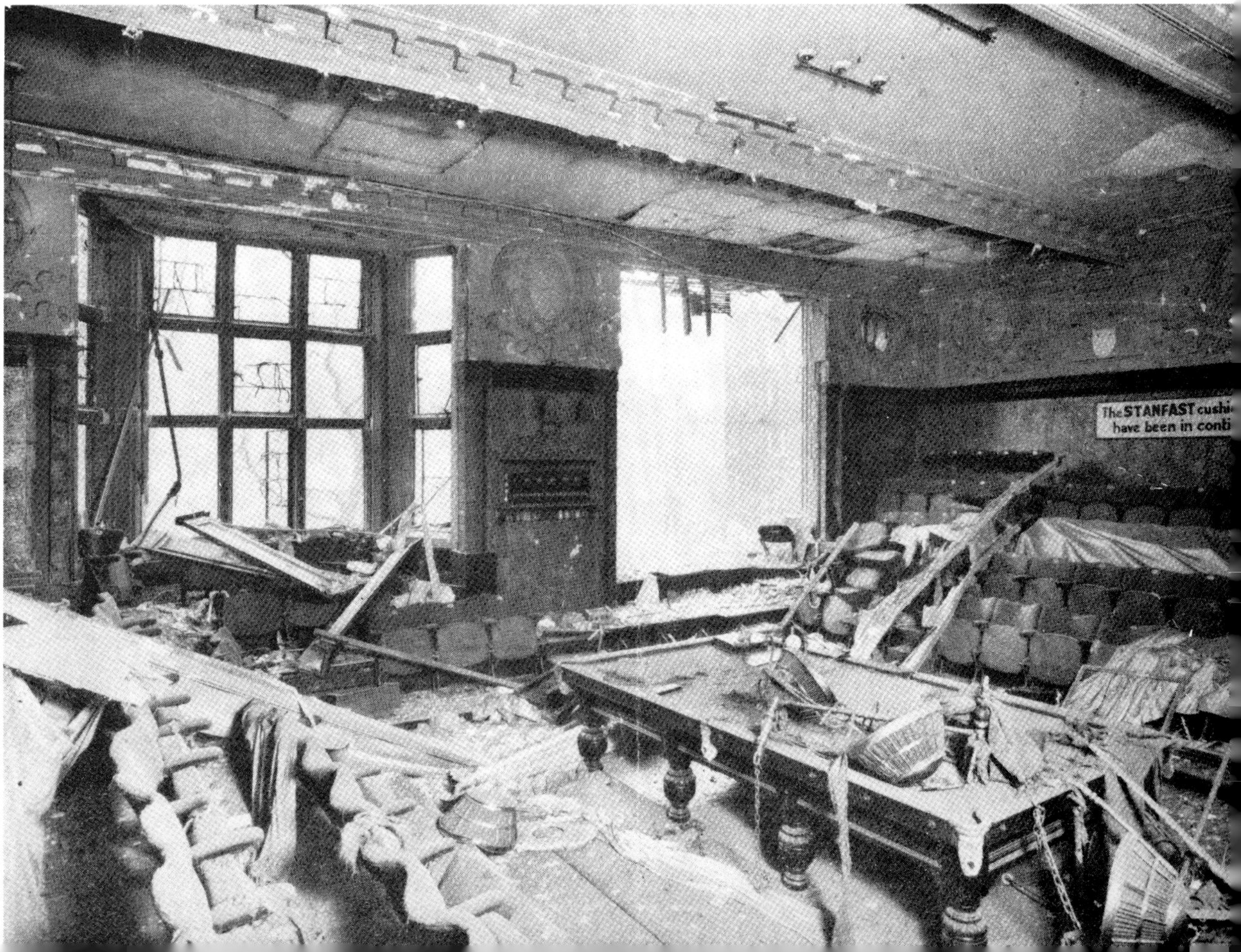

at one time seemed destined to become a stable lad, barman or marker in a billiards hall. But let me put the record straight. I may have been the top man at Leicester Square, but I was the *only* man. I occasionally took the tickets at the box office, made the tea, and continued with one of the chores of my pub days, cleaning the lavatories. In between, I organised the world snooker championships and was thrilled to be in constant touch with stars like Joe and Fred Davis, Horace Lindrum, Walter Donaldson, Alec Brown and Sidney Smith.

We opened the Leicester Square Hall in October 1947. My years there were among the happiest of my life, and 30 January 1955 was a sad night for me, when all my friends of the snooker world turned up for my testimonial and to say goodbye before the famous room I loved so much became part of the huge offices of the Automobile Association, who owned the freehold.

Between 1947 and 1955, as well as dealing with the already established professionals, I made friends with the youngsters who were to step into the shoes of the older stars —players like John Pulman, John Barrie (real name Barrie Smith), Rex Williams, Jack Rea

The newly refurbished and decorated Leicester Square Hall prior to its opening in October 1947.

Leicester Square Hall director Joe Davis checks over a few details with his general manager.

and later, Ray Reardon and John Spencer. These were the new professionals who were to keep the game alive when it slumped so badly in the 1950s and 1960s.

With Joe Davis retired as world champion, it was a quiet, balding Scot named Walter Donaldson, now home from soldiering in the Middle East, who shook the snooker world, becoming the first new world champion since 1927. Also now the shy member of the Davis family, Fred, emerged from the shadow of his more famous brother to win eight world titles, five of them at Leicester Square. Joe himself scored his five hundredth century

Rex Williams, who as a teenager came to Leicester Square as a spectator with his father, made his debut on 10 March 1952.

After winning the title in 1947, Walter Donaldson takes his wife Ida out for a celebration.

Three world champions—Ted with Walter Donaldson, Fred Davis (the current champion) and Joe Davis at a celebration dinner at the Albany Club on 7 May 1948. The champions' wives sit in front of their husbands. This was the first time three world champions were pictured together.

break and went on to score sixty more centuries before the hall closed. And in the last weeks that the hall was open the first officially recognised maximum 147 break was recorded there, causing more excitement even than Walter Lindrum's 4,137 official world record billiards break in 1932.

At Leicester Square, which only seated 200, we had to struggle at times, for there was less money to be earned than there is today—but what fun days they were! It is unfortunate that in snooker, as in other sports, high prize money has increased pressures and tensions on the players and puts too much emphasis on the importance of winning rather than playing. Big money was just not around for the game at Leicester Square, but good-will was abundant. One day a middle-aged man, whom I had never seen before and who wished to remain anonymous, spread one hundred pound notes on my desk and said: 'Mr Lowe, I would like you to give this to the winner of the Joe and Fred Davis match. They have given me so much pleasure watching them'. There was no 'angle' and he didn't even ask to meet the stars—just a splendid sportsman who loved the game. It was not unusual for a businessman to donate £10 or sometimes £20 for any player who made a century during a session. It added to the excitement and brought the best out of the players. A ten-pound note meant something then; and £20 guaranteed a good night on the town.

There always seemed to be time for fun. One lunch-time Leslie Holmes, part of the 'Two Leslies' variety act—Leslie Sarony was the other half—challenged me to a frame. John Pulman and Sydney Lee were present. I had no difficulty in winning because as a snooker player, Leslie was a good pianist. Every time he shaped up to make a shot, John or Syd would make some wisecrack like 'You won't get nowt for that!' Leslie was laughing so much that he went in-off six times in one frame. My main concern was for the safety of the cloth.

At Leicester Square I went out of my way to involve the spectators and to invite one or two personalities from other sports or showbusiness to join the audience. I also organised tournaments and dinners for charities and created the players' first benevolent fund. Annually, I ran a dinner at the Park Lane Hotel on the Sunday after the FA Cup Final and both teams were invited. I was especially thrilled after the famous Stanley Matthews final of 1953 when the old Wizard of Dribble rallied Blackpool from 1-3 down to an incredible 4-3 win with a display that was out of this world. Both Matthews and Stan Mortensen, who scored a hat-trick, came to the dinner as did Nat Lofthouse, the renowned Bolton centre-forward.

I was excited with my new career and strove to give the impression that I knew all the 'in' places in the West End, but I was young and still very much wet behind the ears and my more experienced friends knew it. Leslie Holmes had taken on a new job as publicity manager of the *News of the World* and Joe Davis persuaded that paper to sponsor a £1,500 handicap tournament. One day I was discussing plans with Leslie and two of his directors when one of them said: 'Ted, come and join us for lunch at the big new club just round the corner. It is *the* place at the moment and royalty use it. Of course, you know it!' Rather than confess I was a greenhorn, I muttered: 'Yes, of course!' 'Right', he replied, 'we'll see you round there in ten minutes'.

I had to drag Leslie aside on the pretence of talking business and whispered: 'Which club do they mean?'

'Don't worry, I'll take you there', replied the genial Holmes.

To cut a long story short, Leslie took me through several back streets, then suddenly gave me a quick push into the door of a cafe from which unpleasant smells were escaping. 'Here we are!' he said. And there sitting at a clothless table were the directors, roaring their heads off as they wisecracked: 'Welcome to the Club!' A number of snooker pros will remember the 'Cheap Eatery'!

I was always striving to get sponsorship. Before the war, the *Daily Mail* had backed a Gold Cup tournament which was an outstanding success. As Fred Davis was writing a column in the now defunct *Sunday Empire News*, I asked him to approach that paper about sponsorship. They agreed to put up £1,000 for the first post-war sponsored handicap tournament in August 1948. It was unique in having two handicaps. All the players were handicapped, but a feature that had not been attempted before or since was a sealed envelope with a frame handicap which was not opened until the end of the match. These handicaps were fixed and jealously guarded by the then sports editor, Harold Mayes. It was ironical that the final should come to be decided between Joe and Fred Davis on level terms—in fact, the first time they had met level, surprisingly, Fred won by just one frame. But at the ceremony of the opening of the sealed envelope I was astounded that Mayes had decided that Fred should concede two frames to his brother! It meant that Joe won the tournament and the first prize of £450. Fred ended up taking third prize as John Pulman had already secured second place. Although Joe won, he was not amused. He had always insisted that all opponents must receive at least one black, and to be awarded two frames against Fred annoyed him. There was no *Sunday Empire News* tournament next year. Instead, Joe persuaded the *News of the World* to run their £1,500 tournament which was staged each year from 1949 until Leicester Square closed. Joe played off scratch and no sealed envelopes were allowed.

I set about developing this tournament into an international event and invited George Chenier, the North American champion, from Canada. George arrived with a unique cue which was in two pieces. He also set up a new world record break of 144 at Leicester Square, which was such a challenge to Joe Davis that three weeks later at Manchester Joe made a break of 146 against Chenier. Incidentally, the Canadian brought with him the jazziest set of American ties I had ever seen. When he went back to Canada, he was wearing a sober English tie and had passed on some fifty ornamental neck-ties which finished up in Ted Lowe's wardrobe. I was disappointed that George never returned to Britain.

I also tempted Peter Mans, the South African champion, to come to London. Peter was the father of Perrie Mans, who won Pot Black in 1977 and finished in the final of the 1978 world championships. I found Peter to be a strange character. He was introverted and did

French Canadian George Chenier shows off his two-piece cue. In recent years other players introduced the two-piece cue as something new!

Peter Mans, father of modern South African star Perrie Mans, in action against John Pulman.

Conrad Stanbury, one of the earliest Canadians to make a name in Britain and one of the hardest hitters of a ball ever seen. Tragically, Stanbury eventually had both legs amputated.

not fit in too well with the rest of the boys. One could only describe him as a complete loner. He was a good player and I was sorry he only made one visit, having gone home in a huff after his one trip. Peter and I clashed from the start even though I had done my best to make him welcome. I recall one day when Conrad Stanbury, the veteran Canadian, went down with lumbago. I phoned Mans asking him to help me out of a hole but he was reluctant to take Stanbury's place against John Barrie, saying he wanted to visit the Tower of London. I was fuming and told him he could visit the Tower any day during the next few weeks but it took a great deal of persuading before he agreed to postpone his sight-seeing. Soon we were to become involved in rows. The worst occurred after the referee disqualified him against Sidney Smith for two deliberate misses. Peter was upset, arguing that over the years these tactics had been accepted and were legitimate. However, in Britain we still consider a deliberate miss to be a form of gamemanship not quite in the spirit of the game, and there is still controversy when a referee decides to penalise a player for these tactics.

Feeling he had had a raw deal, Peter protested to the Billiards Association and Control Council against the referee's decision. The controlling body sat on the fence and suggested that as neither the players nor the referee had acted strictly according to the rules, the game should be played again. But I would not agree, insisting that Peter had signed a contract with me which included a clause that he would accept all referees' decisions. I have always believed that in sport players must accept the verdict of the arbiter, even if the referee in question makes an honest error. Once you allow players to reverse a referee's decision, sportsmanship is taken over by gamesmanship.

Peter Mans took grave exception to my stand, pointing out he had won his case for a replay and that I was now the only person obstructing him. When I remained adamant, he hardly spoke to me again apart from assuring me that he intended to cut his English tour short and was not prepared to play two extra matches I had arranged for him to play against George Chenier and Sidney Smith. He made it clear he would not be coming back to Britain. I never saw Peter again. It was a pity because with stronger competition he could have become a better player.

Horace Lindrum was another overseas attraction in that first £1,500 tournament, but was not happy to receive 13 points a frame from Walter Donaldson and 20 points from Joe Davis. However, I felt justified, despite Horace's protests, because Joe once more responded to the challenge and won the £500 first prize playing off scratch. Over six years this

Alec Brown toasts his wife Maureen in September 1949. Joining in the celebration are, from left to right, Horace Lindrum, Sidney Smith, George Chenier, Arthur Goundrill and Joe Davis.

A galaxy of snooker stars at Leicester Square Hall in 1952. Left to right are Willie Smith, Rex Williams, Kingsley Kennerley, Alec Brown, Jack Rea, Sidney Smith, John Barrie, Joe Davis, John Pulman, Walter Donaldson, Sydney Lee, Jim Lees and Fred Davis.

Happy birthday, dear Ted . . . Sidney Smith, Joe Davis, John Pulman and Fred Davis get together before play on Ted's birthday on 1 November 1951.

tournament was also won by Alec Brown, Sidney Smith, Joe Davis for a second time, John Pulman and Jack Rea.

Forever searching for sponsors or gimmicks to attract publicity and new customers for the game, I staged a stunt which brought plenty of publicity in 1948. It was a challenge of non-stop snooker. There was always a lull after Christmas and I got talking to a jeweller-cum-watchmaker who was nuts about the game. He wanted to play for forty-eight hours non-stop at Leicester Square. I wondered what reaction there would be to this marathon in the holy of holies but, with nothing to lose, we went ahead. I invited my friends, the sports editors and columnists from Fleet Street, to take turns in the marathon and took the precaution of seeing that a St John's Ambulance nurse was always on hand. The name of the marathon king was perfect for Fleet Street. It was Dickie Flicker. (And I'm not kidding.) He was a member of the Beaufort Club in Lisle Street, a hot-bed of snooker aspirants and a meeting place for the professionals and stage stars. Dickie stuck to his guns. At times we took his shoes and socks off and bathed his feet in brandy. Sometimes he played in his socks. We kept him going with sandwiches and flasks of black coffee. I had him checked by a doctor. Dickie completed 141 frames and played non-stop for two days and two nights but was completely shattered at the end. I had strapped a pedometer to his ankle. It worked out he walked nearly three miles in each frame.

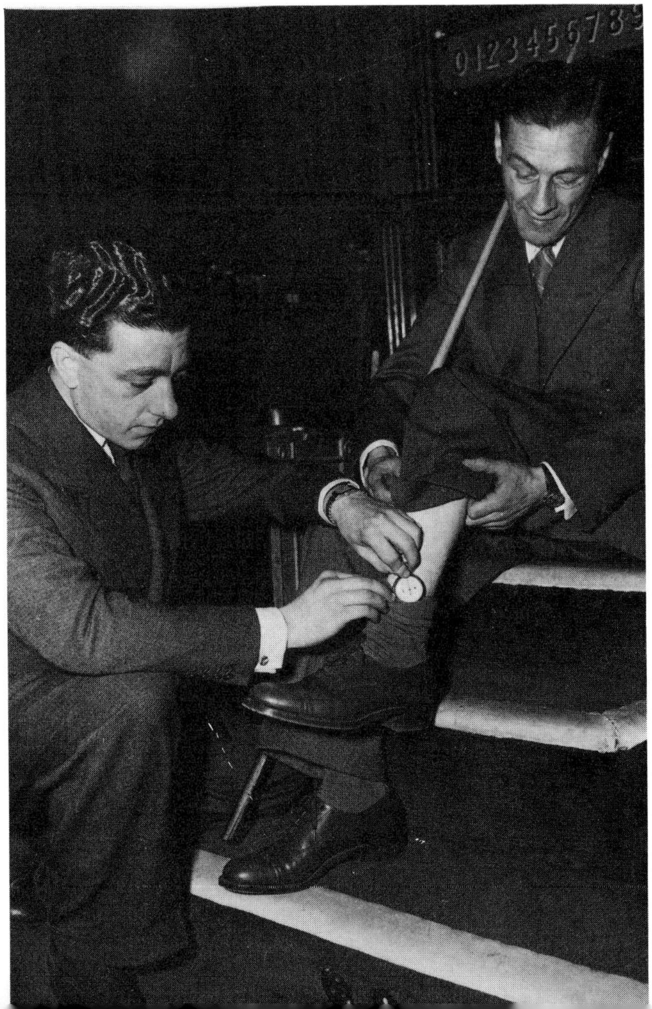

Fixing a pedometer in the sock of Dickie Flicker, the snooker 'nut' who took part in a marathon at Leicester Square Hall in 1948.

Fortunately for us, the weather at this time was bad. Racing and football had been postponed and the sports editors were glad to have something to fill empty pages. Dickie Flicker's picture was all over the sports pages. As I had promoted the event, I felt obliged to be on duty night and day. One night after Peter Wilson of the *Daily Mirror* had played a frame against Flicker, Peter and I retired to my office after midnight and opened a bottle of Scotch. Peter was a great character who, in his younger days, never wanted to go to bed. We saw the dawn arrive in my office and a second bottle of Scotch was demolished. Tired as we were, when Peter hailed a cab to go home to breakfast, we looked in far better shape than Dickie, still walking round the table playing wearily against another man from Fleet Street.

We also had a great drive at this time to promote the women's game. In 1948 the Women's Billiards Association had an enthusiastic and beautiful president in the actress Valerie Hobson, who had made such a hit starring in *The King and I* at Drury Lane, and who used to play with radio star Lynn Joyce. There were some more than useful women players around. Thelma Carpenter, then the reigning champion, Joyce Gardner and Ruth Harrison, who was snooker champion several times and in my opinion the best woman player I've seen, made great efforts to revive interest by running professional billiards and snooker championships, which had been done since the early 1930s but had lapsed with the war. We also tried putting on matches between Joyce, Thelma and Ruth at Leicester Square, but unfortunately the ladies did not attract worthwhile audiences at that time.

Valerie Hobson presents the trophy to Ruth Harrison.

Valerie admiring the trophy with Thelma Carpenter, Joyce Gardner and Agnes Morris (now Davies).

Another first promotion were the foursome challenge matches between Joe Davis and Walter Donaldson, representing the *News of the World,* and Fred Davis and John Pulman for the *Evening News.*

Thurston's had been modernised without intruding on its tradition and intimacy. The room was renowned for its decorative murals. Music was introduced during the intervals. Patrons always tip-toed and dared not move or cough when one of the maestros was in the middle of a big break. With snooker gaining popularity immediately after the war, I introduced a ten- or fifteen-minute interval after three frames had been played and although there was no bar, everybody welcomed the chance to stretch their legs or discuss

Leicester Square Hall never had a drink licence so John Pulman and Joe Davis have fun. John takes a cup of tea and Joe chooses a tomato juice.

the games among themselves and elderly gentlemen breathed a sigh of relief as they enjoyed the second three frames in more comfort than in the days when Thurston's had no intervals.

There was one occasion I shall never forget. I was sitting in my office preparing for an afternoon session between John Pulman and John Barrie when the phone rang. A man inquired if it was possible for me to arrange an exhibition match between two professionals for the opening of a new West End club. Normally, that was no problem for me but I was taken back when, on asking what sort of date the stranger had in mind, he replied: 'Tonight!' 'That's a tall order at short notice', I gasped. But bearing in mind how little money there was in the game at this time, I continued the conversation, explaining that there was a possibility that when John Pulman and John Barrie arrived they might be interested but I would want to know what fee was involved. He said he would pay £100 and the club was in Upper St Martin's Lane, not more than a long pot from Leicester Square. Any time from 10pm onwards would do.

The two Johns jumped at the offer. A hundred pounds may sound chickenfeed now but professionals were lucky to pick up £5 or £10 for an exhibition then. So £100 split between the three of us seemed good pay for an hour's work.

The session at Leicester Square that night was just about the shortest held during my spell as manager. Pulman and Barrie began at the normal time of 7.30pm. It was all over by 9 o'clock. They broke the pyramid at the start of each frame and played like men with a plane to catch, balls disappearing in all pockets. At the end we had a quick beer before setting off for the club in John Pulman's small Hillman Minx.

When we arrived at the address it all seemed very strange. We walked through the front door into a room with about a dozen small tables, each with a telephone and nothing else. I pushed open another door and saw a crowd of men and women chatting and drinking. I found my way to the bar, introduced myself and inquired if the character who made the phone call was available as John Pulman and John Barrie were ready to play an exhibition.

This was the man who had telephoned, and he asked what we would like to drink first. I told him Pulman would have a gin and tonic, Barrie a Scotch and I would have a half pint of beer. He seemed friendly enough, though I was surprised when he handed me a tray holding a bottle of gin, a bottle of Scotch and a pint of beer. He told us to take a seat and promised to call us soon. We sat sipping our drinks for some twenty minutes and nothing happened, so I went back to the bar to tell the man we were in a hurry, saying that we had another engagement later, and would he like to settle the £100 fee as he had agreed. He immediately produced the fee in £1 notes, which I put into my pocket, returning to our table to tell the boys: 'Well, at least we've been paid. The geezer has promised to give us a shout in another ten minutes.'

Another half-an-hour passed and the situation was getting ridiculous, so it was my lot to give the man another reminder. 'O.K.', he said, 'I'll take you through to the billiards room.' What followed was unbelievable. We went through the room with the small tables and telephones into an even smaller room, empty apart from a table that was no bigger than three feet long and a foot wide! We were so astounded that we didn't know whether to laugh or get angry. If he had not already paid up we would certainly have walked out. I was not sure whether we were being set up by a practical joker, but said: 'My dear fellow, you can't expect professionals to play snooker on a toy table; but as you have paid, they will play 30 up at billiards, but where is the audience?'

He did not quibble, but replied: 'You can start now. People will come in later.' But only one man arrived and it was difficult for us to keep straight faces. Pulman broke and Barrie made a few cannons and in-offs. It was so absurd that after fifteen minutes the three of us walked out and not a word was said. Outside the club we were doubled up with laughter at the crazy session but as we had £100, decided to go to Hatchett's in Piccadilly for a celebration. While we were laughing, two regular fans from Leicester Square joined us and we made for Hatchett's but as Pulman's car wouldn't hold five, John Barrie—the tallest at 6 foot 3 inches—sat astride the bonnet, and that's how we went through Leicester Square and along Piccadilly.

We left in the early hours, and again Barrie sat astride the bonnet. It was two-way traffic then and John Pulman deliberately jammed his foot on the brake as we reached Leicester Square Hall; Barrie, of course, went over the front of the bonnet. That was the end of a

On a visit to Streatham Ice Rink, John Barrie in ice hockey gear tries an unlikely cannon.

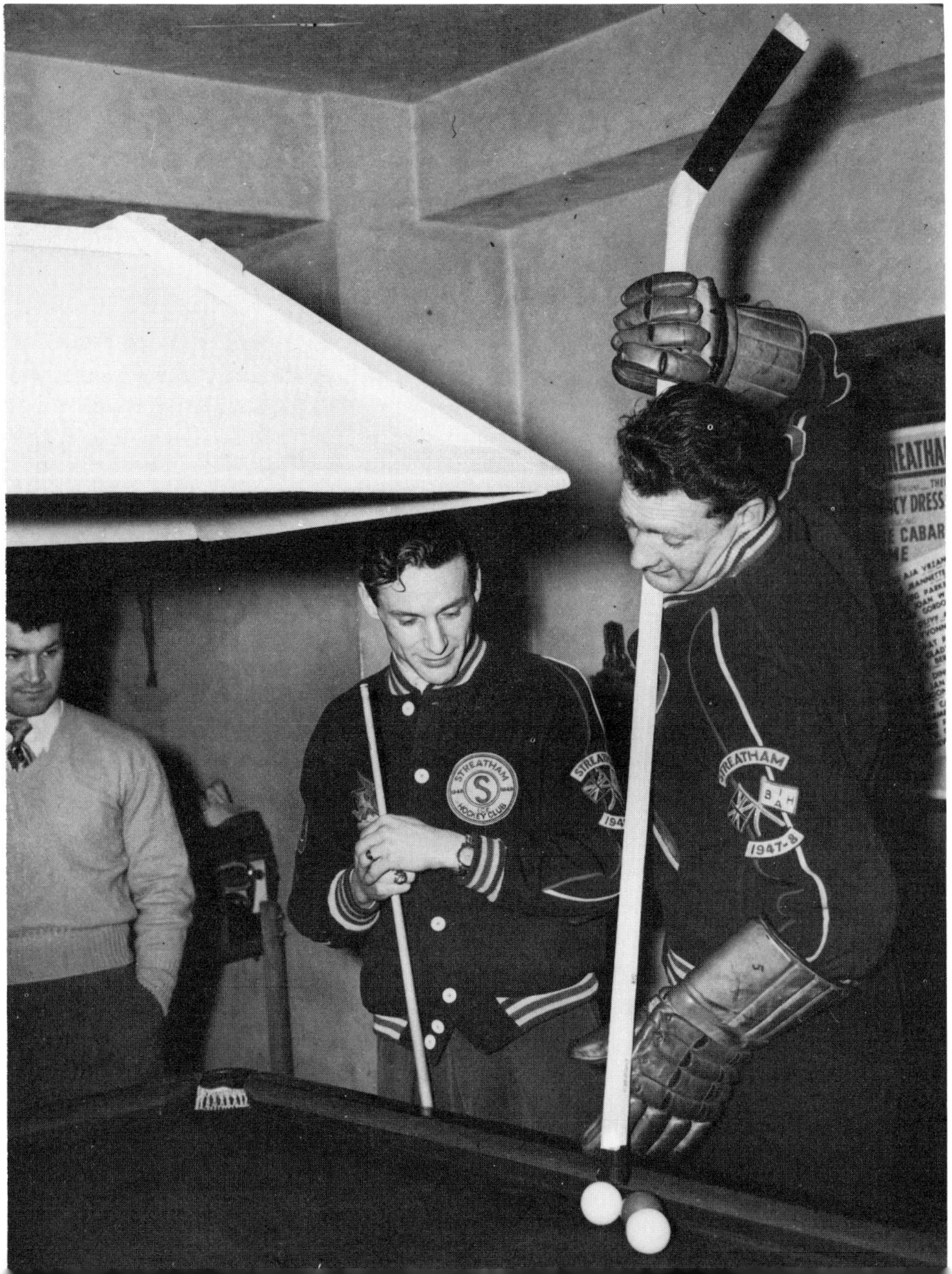

very funny evening—the sort of episode that none of us, now much older and wiser, would or could attempt today.

Needless to say, the club we had visited was closed by the police a couple of days later. Obviously, the invitation to play a snooker exhibition had been a front for what must have been a gaming club, betting shop or even call-girls. It had been clear to us that nobody was in the least interested in snooker.

The King and I. A proud moment posing with the world's greatest player.

Mind you, it wasn't always such fun. Many a night Bruce Donkin—who obtained his Grade A Referees' Certificate at the same time as myself—and I had dreary journeys home on the Tube. We were both hard up, and taxis were out of the question. Nevertheless, those were the days, my friend, we thought would never end. But, alas, all good things do come to an end.

The night of 30 January 1955 is one I shall always remember. It was the night the final curtain came down on Leicester Square Hall. At last I had to face what I knew was inevitable: for me, it was Farewell Leicester Square. Even if I had been able to foresee the next thirty years and the amazing rise in popularity of the game after the doldrums of the late 1950s and the 1960s, I think I would still have felt that the world of snooker would never be quite the same for me after that famous match room—first opened in 1901, bombed in 1940, re-opened and re-styled in 1947—had gone forever.

The last match staged at Leicester Square was between Joe and Fred Davis, before an invited audience including the Duke of Roxburghe, President of the Professional Billiards Players Association, on 29 January 1955. Joe and Fred had opened the Leicester Square Hall in 1947; it was fitting that they should close it. The final frame was seen by millions through television.

Ted's testimonial night at Leicester Square Hall on 30 January 1955. All the greats raise a smile on a sad occasion. From left to right: Jack Rea, Sidney Smith, Fred Davis, Sydney Lee, Arthur Goundrill, Claude Falkiner, John Pulman, Ted Lowe, Joe Davis, Alec Brown, Willie Smith and Horace Lindrum.

But 30 January was *my* night, before the doors were to close for the last time on that little room that seated just under two hundred spectators. It was my testimonial night, and every professional turned up to take part. I was deeply moved by their friendship and I still treasure the magnificent silver salver presented to me by Joe Davis.

The closing of the hall was not the end of snooker, but it was a terrible blow to the professional side of the game which almost died as a spectator sport over the next fifteen or so years.

Such had been the tranquillity in the hall, with its almost monastic atmosphere, that J.B. Priestley had written way back in 1929:

> 'When the world is wrong, hardly to be endured, I shall return to Thurston's Hall and there smoke a pipe among the connoisseurs of top and side. It is as near to the Isle of Innisfree as we can get within a hundred leagues of Leicester Square'.

Perhaps Yeats would not have appreciated the comparison between Thurston's and Innisfree, but the peace of the place must have made a deep impression on 'J.B.'

I was sad enough, but Joe Davis and Sidney Smith, who had been directors under Bob Jelks and had played so many great matches there, were misty-eyed when Sidney recalled a night in December 1936, playing against Tom Newman in the *Daily Mail* Gold Cup. As the

Sidney Smith (left) and Albert Brown, two regulars at Leicester Square Hall. When it closed both these fine players retired and never reappeared on the snooker scene.

clock struck nine Sidney had potted the final black to set up a new world record break of 133 and had taken every ball, fifteen reds and six colours to clear the table. Immediately, everybody gathered round a radio which had been set up in the room to hear the sad and historic farewell speech of King Edward VIII telling of his abdication from the throne in order to marry Mrs Simpson and to become the exiled Duke of Windsor.

We sat up into the early hours of the morning indulging in nostalgia as that great old-timer Willie Smith talked of the days at the beginning of the century when as a young man, having defeated Tom Newman, he was matched against the much-feared billiards star of the day, H.W. Stevenson. Willie was given a 3,000 start in a 9,000 points match but finished up beating the great man by well over 3,000. Harry Stevenson was not amused.

Memories are great, but they don't feed a man and his family and I was now out of work, though the money raised from the farewell night was more than enough to satisfy my immediate needs. It was only now that I realised how hard I had played as well as worked and on the advice of my doctor took a three months' holiday to wind down. I found myself enjoying this new life of leisure but a good friend gave me some sound advice. 'You're too

Willie Smith, one of the great billiards veterans, celebrates his sixty-eighth birthday on 25 January 1954, with a match of mixed billiards and snooker against Joe Davis. A year later Joe scored the first official maximum 147 break against Willie.

young and not rich enough to do nothing. Laziness can become a habit. It's better to wear out than rust away. Get back to work'. Though a part of me seemed to have died, I realised my friend was talking sense and although I had turned down an offer from Ind Coope to run a small hotel, I decided to contact them again and see if they could use me in some capacity—though I was determined not to turn my back on the game which always was and always will be part of my life. So I offered myself as a salesman and was granted an interview with two directors.

Once again my life was to be changed. It was only the second full-time job I was to hold and the first time I had to face an interview for employment. With snooker in mind, I decided to take along my scrapbook to the interview. The move paid off. The interview lasted an hour and the conversation was more about snooker than beer, but in order to sell beer I had to sell myself to the directors first. They must have been reasonably impressed because they appointed me there and then and, more important to me, it was agreed that my snooker and showbiz contacts would be an asset in my new job and it was written into my contract that I would be allowed to continue to keep up my full interest in the game.

What luck! Here I was, one minute out of one job and believing my world of snooker had crashed. Now I had a new job, far more lucrative than I could have dreamed of, and the bonus of being encouraged to continue my involvement in snooker. And even though, without its old shop-window, snooker was heading for a thin time tournament-wise, I had many contacts with clubs and, just as it seemed that billiards and beer went hand in hand when I worked in the family pub at Lambourn, I now found that snooker was to bring me plenty of orders for beer in my new job.

Ind Coope was to become the largest drinks group in Europe and the largest beer manufacturer in Great Britain, with its mergers with household names like Benskin and Friary in the South, Ansell's in the Midlands and Tetley's in the North, and later with Joe Lyons to form the great Allied-Lyons conglomerate. Apart from playing more snooker than I had for seven or eight years in the clubs of south-east London, I found myself getting promotion first as personal assistant followed by London sales manager, South England sales manager, and finally as director of National Account Sales for the United Kingdom in 1973. I was now responsible for selling literally millions of pints of beer to groups like Sainsbury, Tesco, Grand Met, British Rail, Trust House Forte, Butlins, Pontins, NAAFI and all the airlines.

I still missed Leicester Square Hall and was saddened by the demise of the world championships and the big matches, but I was happy with my success in the commercial world. Although I have now retired from Allied Breweries, I was again fortunate in 1979. The chairman of Queen's Moat Houses PLC invited me to join his board of directors and in my autumn years I use my off duty snooker thoughts in the pleasing way of offering what assistance I can to that highly successful hotel group.

Ted and brewery colleague Bill McCarthy pose on the roof of Allied House before another day at 'Royal Ascot'.

CHAPTER 2

Downs–and Ups

I HAD no financial problems in 1955. Yet though I now had new fields to conquer I asked myself: 'What is to become of snooker without its shop window?' Only a handful of professionals felt secure and with our headquarters gone there was a grave danger of us drifting apart.

The war had seen the billiard table removed from the pubs; the space was more profitably employed as a drinking area. Clubs in the main had retained their billiard room but this was for members only and, in any case, mostly too small to seat big enough audiences to attract professionals.

The few players around knew the suitable venues up and down the country, but with no sponsors, and very few promoters with sufficient cash, things looked bleak. I remember staging a quarter-final heat in the world championship between Horace Lindrum and Herbert Holt, then Northern snooker champion, in a small Nissen hut club in Streatham owing to the lack of a better place to play it. The gate money embarrassed both of them.

Joe Davis had taught himself to become a sound businessman and had wisely invested his earnings. Fred and his wife had their hotel. Sidney Smith had bought a delightful new home on the river in the Thames Valley and did not seem worried about his future. Alec Brown had gone back to his first love of motor bikes and their engines, while Walter Donaldson was happy on his small farm in Bedfordshire. But what of younger players like John Pulman, John Barrie and Jack Rea? How would they make a living out of the game? And did snooker have any future as a spectator sport if no new blood was coming along?

One of my regrets is that I completely lost touch with Sidney Smith. He was not only a fine player and a director of Leicester Square but a splendid person. Sidney clearly made up his mind to get right out of snooker. I often wonder what became of him.

Alec Brown was one player who decided to retire from professional snooker. He was then forty-seven and had had a colourful career. At fifteen he was the Jimmy White of his day. A deadly potter, he became a billiards marker at the Ritz Hotel and, while still in his teens, rode in TT races on the Isle of Man. He was mechanically minded and clever with his hands despite suffering from chronic arthritis from an early age. Alec made big snooker news before the war, winning the Daily Mail Gold Cup in 1938 and 1939. After the war he

Alec Brown presents a silver cigarette box to Ted in appreciation of all the help given him. He was the only player who made this gesture.

won the Albany Club tournament in 1950 and the News of the World £1,500 handicap the following year. He reached the semi-finals of the world championships in 1936, 1938 and 1954. Yet Alec Brown is still most remembered by old-timers for introducing a 'Fountain Pen' cue to make a difficult shot. It caused a sensation at the time when Alec proved there was no law against it, and the controlling body were forced to bring in a new rule so that a cue today must be at least three feet in length.

In his last bid for the world title in 1955, when he was beaten in the semi-final by John Pulman, Alec played with both wrists strapped to ease the pain of increasing arthritis. He had married Maureen Crosby, one of the secretaries at the Billiards Association, and they moved to Plymouth where they still live. Alec returned to working on racing engines and set about building a sports car from scratch. At sixty-nine his arthritis became so severe that he had to have all his toes amputated. He accepted the ordeal and after months in hospital

Alec Brown with his 'Fountain Pen' cues.

learning to walk again he and Maureen went off for a long holiday in Yugoslavia. Such was his fighting spirit that he was able to walk again, dance and tackle Plymouth Hoe though his feet are two sizes smaller.

During 1955 I continued to plead with the BBC to run a series on television, suggesting that Joe Davis give exhibitions against one of the top professionals, demonstrating some of his fascinating trick shots. But the BBC, like the Press, could see no future in snooker and, apart from putting on a couple of programmes consisting of perhaps ten minutes, the game did not interest them.

I had helped to form the Professional Billiards Players Association, and twelve months earlier put together the original Referees Association which was founded to support the professionals in some of their differences with the Billiards Association and Control Council, a very autocratic body. I am delighted to say that the present ruling body—the Billiards and Snooker Control Council—is a far more democratic and friendly association. As I happen to be its President, what else can I say! Joe Davis was the first chairman of the Players Association, Alec Brown the vice-chairman, and the Duke of Roxburghe accepted our invitation to become President. I took on the more arduous task of honorary organising secretary. We had eighteen professional members plus three ladies, Agnes Morris, Joyce Gardner and Thelma Carpenter. Only two top-class players declined to join, Clark McConachy and Horace Lindrum.

The Billiards Association and Control Council disapproved of the formation of the Players Association. They didn't like the professionals having any say in the game, and

Clark McConachy, New Zealand's greatest billiards and snooker player, says farewell to London in 1953. At Waterloo station he presents his set of billiards balls to John Weedon, a young porter. Clark held the world billiards title undefended for seventeen years.

The chores of the champions. Walter Donaldson and John Pulman seem happy enough signing autographs for fans after a match.

when in 1952 only those two players, who had not joined the Players Association, entered the world championships sponsored by the B.A. & C.C., the rest of the professionals boycotted the event. Lindrum beat McConachy at Manchester and claimed the title, but the professionals who did not compete never accepted him as world champion. In the same year Fred Davis beat Walter Donaldson to win the world title for the fourth time in six years, the Scot having won it twice. Fred went on to beat John Pulman and took eight world championships before announcing his retirement. There was so little cash around in snooker at that time that no-one could blame Fred for deciding to retire from tournament play and only take part in exhibitions if the fee was worthwhile. His wife Sheila was running a hotel in North Wales and there was obviously no future in Fred travelling round the country not earning enough to cover his expenses. Fortunately, Fred returned to competitive snooker for Pot Black, the world championships and other major tournaments when the game began to pick up again.

John Pulman sets off on his first overseas trip—to South Africa—in April 1954, on the *Athlone Castle* boat train.

Pulman's wife Frankie welcomes him home at the end of the trip.

John Pulman must be given credit for battling on and keeping an interest in the world championships through these most difficult years, in which the professionals were left to organise the championships themselves. In 1957, with Fred Davis deciding not to defend, John Pulman, Rex Williams, Jack Rea and Kingsley Kennerley took part in the championships in Jersey and Pulman won his first title, beating Jack Rea in the final. Pulman kept as busy as possible, but such was the lack of interest that no world championships were organised between 1958 and 1963. Then, following a truce with the B.A. & C.C., the world champion was allowed to defend his title against a challenge from a single player. Pulman, like a boxing champion, put up his crown against all comers and from 1964 to 1968 successfully defended it seven times, beating Fred Davis three times, Rex Williams twice, Freddie van Rensburg and Eddie Charlton. Pulman had a tremendous run—very gratifying for the Devonian who had been beaten by Albert Brown in the qualifying round when he first entered the world championships in 1947, and beaten again by Albert in the quarter finals in 1950.

Jack Warner loved a game of snooker and is seen here watching Bob Jelks, who gave Ted Lowe his break at Leicester Square Hall, in action during a charity match.

A social occasion with Nancy Spain, 'Ena Sharples' of Coronation Street and Freddie Mills.

Another function of the Players Association was to raise funds for professionals who might fall on hard times, and although we started in a small way we are proud that the Association has grown into such a healthy and powerful body. Our very first tournament raised only £372 for the funds, but when you remember that in 1982 the Association promoted its first-ever tournament with £50,000 in prize money, you can see that the pioneers started something big.

In the beginning, I had begged, borrowed or otherwise acquired a number of gifts from good friends and well-wishers; and as well as support from all the leading professionals, I had tremendous help from my showbiz friends. The Crazy Gang, Ben Warris, Tommy Trinder, Nat Jackley, Jack Warner, Fred Emney and Charlie Chester were just a few who turned up free of charge for charity matches. Sportsmen like Freddie Mills, Dai Rees, Alf Gover and Joe Mercer all supported me by turning out in any pro-celebrity tournament I ran for the players. I invited wealthy and influential fans to attend, and many generous donations were made which went to established charities like the National Association of Boys Clubs, Home for Incurables, Star and Garter and Cancer Research. I am proud to say that over a few years we donated over £250,000 in different ways, with a good proportion to Cancer Research, through the efforts of the famous surgeon Arthur Dickson-Wright. It was a rewarding way to keep snooker afloat.

Murray's Club and the Albany Club also showed interest in snooker during the bleak years and whenever possible would arrange tournaments or exhibition matches. One night at Murray's we had Joe Davis and Horace Lindrum playing on a table set up on the dance floor with Joyce Gardner commentating. To raise some extra cash for charity I invited all present to gamble a fiver on how long it would take to dismantle the table after the game was finished. It took twenty-two minutes—and several hundred pounds were raised.

Despite all these efforts, it was a tremendous struggle to keep our heads above water and save the game from going under completely. Soccer, boxing and all the other sports seemed to be booming. Snooker was the poor relation in the 1950s and 1960s. But the fight was a good fight—though none of us then could see that at the end of the 1960s snooker was to stage such a come-back that through the 1970s and into the 1980s it was to become more prosperous than any sport. That come-back was due almost entirely to colour television.

THE first chink of light appeared at the end of a very dark and long snooker tunnel in 1969. After years of pestering my BBC contacts to give the game a break on television, out of the blue came a 'phone call from Phillip Lewis, then a producer on BBC2. He asked if I would care to devise a thirty-minute series to run for eight weeks in colour. I just couldn't believe my ears. This was, indeed, manna from Heaven.

BBC2 had not been going for very long and was rather highbrow in its choice of programme, and I must confess I couldn't quite see the game clicking on this channel. However, these were very private thoughts and there was no way I would dare throw any doubts on such a wonderful opportunity. We talked it over and decided that the initial format would consist of a sudden death tournament between two sets of four well-known professionals, with the top two in each group forming the semi-finalists. It was to be recorded over four days at the old Gosta Green studio in Birmingham, immediately after Christmas, and shown to the viewers later.

Thus Pot Black was born at the end of 1969. The title was the brain-child of Phillip Lewis, and I admit I didn't like it at first, thinking that the word 'snooker' should be included. How wrong I was. Mention Pot Black in any part of the world today and you immediately think of snooker. The director of the first programme was Reg Perrin, who has been its producer since 1971. In fact, Reg, who retired in June, 1983, and I were the only two who had been with the series since its inception. It has become the longest running series at the Pebble Mill TV Studio.

I think it fair to say that the seeds of snooker's astounding popularity on television today were sown when Phillip Lewis and I first discussed Pot Black. But I must point out that some of my ideas were frowned on by some professionals who, understandably, did not relish risking their reputations by getting knocked out of a tournament decided on one frame. But it seemed to be a winner from the start, appealing to a completely new audience of TV viewers, many of whom had never even seen the game played before.

Inevitably we had teething troubles, but not only did Pot Black reach a massive new public, it also spawned a new breed of snooker players—mainly youngsters—who were not only fascinated by mastering the skills of the game but who realised that they could become wealthy personalities, and as famous as the pop stars of the sixties. It was estimated that nearly one million people watched that first series. This figure trebled within three years and snooker today can probably boast of an audience of sixteen million for one of the top finals.

The timing for the launch of a new TV tournament was perfect. We had seen Fred Davis and John Pulman dominate the scene in the 1950s and 1960s, but now three very good amateurs—Ray Reardon, John Spencer and Gary Owen—had turned professional and there was no doubt new blood was needed if the game was to boom. It all worked out splendidly for me, having pressed for the newcomers rather than only established professionals. Pot Black's first winner was Reardon with Spencer the runner-up. Ray also made the highest break with 99. In the same year John won his first world title, beating Gary Owen in the final. Then Ray Reardon took the world crown in the spring of 1970 and when it was competed for again in the winter of the same year in Australia, it was recaptured by Spencer.

The new boys seemed to excel at Pot Black. Apart from Reardon's first win, it was taken over by Spencer in 1970 and in 1971 and suddenly snooker had a whole lot of new faces. Our policy was to keep looking for a fresh name and to try and find a dark-horse winner. This in itself involved me in many controversies and rows with some more established professionals who clearly did not like my leaving them out. I believe I justified my selections by the number of shock winners Pot Black produced, which included Eddie Charlton from Australia, Graham Miles, the South African Perrie Mans, and Doug Mountjoy.

It was my idea to bring in an international flavour by inviting Eddie Charlton to take part in 1972. Although an all-round athlete, Eddie did not take up snooker seriously until he was thirty. However, he not only won Pot Black in his first attempt, but repeated his win in 1973 and became the second player to win the event three times when he beat Reardon in 1980. It was Eddie's triumph in 1972 that caused a snooker TV revolution in Australia, where they booked the series to be screened coast to coast; later came the Winfield tournament which involved me in flying 'Down Under' once a year as the commentator.

However, a great deal of hard work and heartache were involved before we were to achieve lasting success. Pot Black began very modestly in an old cinema at Gosta Green, Birmingham, entirely as an experiment for colour television. Reg Perrin and Jim

Dumigham of the BBC and myself as the commentator were mainly responsible for inviting eight players. In the first series, they agreed to share equally and each player received £244. Today with overseas royalties the kitty is £41,000. And they are still demanding more!

Two hundred and forty-four pounds may not sound much cash, but remember that snooker was not flourishing in 1969; there were not more than eight professionals making a good full-time living from the game and not more than three could claim they were topping £10,000 a year. For that initial recording the BBC had to scrape around to find enough people—including cleaners and the canteen staff—to fill the seats in the cinema to give the programme the right atmosphere. Today at Pebble Mill the luxurious studio seats 300 people and the BBC have a waiting list of up to 10,000. In order to give the competitors more cash, we experimented with the programme, reducing the number of players to six in 1972, but went back to eight the following year. This was the ideal number for that format. By 1978 the prize money had increased, with the winner collecting £1,000, and it caused some embarrassment when we decided to leave out Fred Davis, Rex Williams, Dennis Taylor and John Pulman. We did our best to be fair by including five previous winners: John Spencer, Ray Reardon, Eddie Charlton, Graham Miles and the 1977 winner Perrie Mans. We made up the eight by inviting Cliff Thorburn and Doug Mountjoy and recalling Alex Higgins, who had not been included since 1972 and whose omission had caused much controversy.

We had invited Alex Higgins to take part after he gained the world title at his first attempt in 1972. I did not realise what sort of headache I had let myself in for! The unpredictable Irishman was beaten in his first frame and immediately protested against the whole system of Pot Black, declaring forcibly how crazy it was to decide a match on one frame. He also objected strongly at having to wait around for television producers, directors and crew, and did not like the cameras at this stage. He told me bluntly that he did not intend to hang around any more for this particular series. With fifteen matches still to be filmed, the powers-that-be became very annoyed with the Hurricane's attitude. Audiences had been arranged for the next three days, cash had been spent setting up the series, and the studio had been especially set aside for the recordings as most other programmes consisted of dramas. I took part in a drama of my own, sitting up all night with the unhappy Alex in a Birmingham hotel striving to talk him round to take part in a second game. Finally, in the small hours of the morning, after all the other pros had tried a little persuasion, Alex reluctantly agreed to play, but he did not finish among the prizewinners.

Though Higgins continued to play well in other tournaments, the BBC declined to invite him back to Pot Black for a long time; many protests were made on his behalf by snooker fans but the BBC were firm. Alex also made himself unpopular in Australia and he was not included in the sixteen players invited to compete in the world match-play championship in Melbourne in 1979—a previous visit by the Hurricane had ended in a brush with the law.

Alex Higgins was, and still is, magic at the box-office. I suggested we should give him another chance in 1975 but then he got himself mixed up in some very bad publicity which ended with him spending a night in jail. So the invitation for the Prodigal Son to return and taste of the fatted calf was further delayed. Alex's fans took up his cause and letters were published in the magazine *Snooker Scene* in 1976. One Worcester reader accused the BBC of prejudice against Higgins, describing him as the 'greatest personality in the game with a touch of genius'. *Snooker Scene* invited Reg Perrin to reply on behalf of the BBC and Reg obliged thus:

Away from the billiard table as most men were during 1939-45, Sydney Lee as a war-reserve policeman still found time to practise in the billiards room at the police station.

> Decisions regarding the invitation of eight players to take part in Pot Black are made annually in conjunction with Ted Lowe, the programme's commentator, and the WPSBA committee. Many factors are taken into account but the overriding consideration is the success of the programme itself. This, today, no longer depends necessarily upon the participation of any individual player. Disappointed professionals have accepted this fact gracefully.
>
> The future progress of the game is the constant aim of all those connected with Pot Black. It may not be generally known that the series has been seen in Australia, Tasmania, New Zealand, Hong Kong, Borneo and Eire. We are proud to be instrumental in advancing the careers of, among others, Graham Miles, Dennis Taylor and Willie Thorne. Again Ray Reardon won the first Pot Black trophy in 1969 before becoming world champion. Your correspondent's interest and concern for Pot Black's future is greatly appreciated but accusations such as 'banned', 'punished' and 'vendetta' are not accepted by this office as possessing validity.

Alex had to wait until Pot Black 1978 to be invited again. I was particularly sorry that year to leave out Fred Davis, but Fred was the first to agree with me that Higgins should be included despite his earlier lapse. However, in 1979 we not only invited a twenty-one-year-old Plumstead boy named Steve Davis to take part but brought Fred Davis back at sixty-five. This caused yet more controversy—how could Ted Lowe prefer an old age pensioner to Alex Higgins? But the matter is not one of personal preference, but that one-frame snooker does not really suit the Hurricane, and while he made a great come-back to win the world championship in 1982, ten years after his first victory, he won't look back on Pot Black as one of his favourite tournaments.

Those of us involved with it look upon Pot Black as greater than any of its individual competitors, including its champions.*

It has gone from success to success, and has set a standard for richer tournaments. Not only have we introduced new names, but the players dress like film stars. And most professionals accept that Pot Black came to the rescue just in time.

Another who dressed immaculately was my old friend Sydney Lee. One of my greatest

---

**Pot Black Winners*

	Winner	*Runner-up*
1969	Ray Reardon	John Spencer
1970	John Spencer	Ray Reardon
1971	John Spencer	Fred Davis
1972	Eddie Charlton	Ray Reardon
1973	Eddie Charlton	Rex Williams
1974	Graham Miles	John Spencer
1975	Graham Miles	Dennis Taylor
1976	John Spencer	Dennis Taylor
1977	Perrie Mans	Doug Mountjoy
1978	Doug Mountjoy	Graham Miles
1979	Ray Reardon	Doug Mountjoy
1980	Eddie Charlton	Ray Reardon
1981	Cliff Thorburn	Jim Wych
1982	Steve Davis	Eddie Charlton
1983	Steve Davis	Ray Reardon

pleasures was to be able to recommend Syd to act as referee for Pot Black in 1970. A superb billiards and snooker player, Syd had spent thirty-five years as resident professional and coach at Burroughes and Watts in Soho Square. When the hall was closed down through lack of interest no-one was sadder than Syd. He had never been a referee but knew every aspect of the game and I had no hesitation in recommending him. And what a success he made of the job. The man who had thrilled crowds before and after the war was the perfect, elegant and authoritative referee as, in his white gloves, he unobtrusively controlled the games. Because of television Sydney Lee became a better known personality in ten years as a referee than in thirty-five years as a brilliant player. He retired in 1980 through ill health and was thrilled when we presented him with the Pot Black Personality Trophy and his friends in the game staged a testimonial night for him at the Berkshire Club at Windsor.

Like myself, Syd was born in a pub, the King William IV at Streatham. He won the English boys billiards title at fourteen, was English amateur champion at twenty, and world amateur champion in 1933 and 1934. He played in Australia and became a friend of Walter Lindrum. He joined the pros in 1934 and while his game was billiards, he realised that snooker was the game of the future and adapted himself to it with great skill. But the winning of the world snooker title was almost impossible because of that man Joe Davis—Syd confirms my belief that Joe was the greatest. Syd and his wife Gladys, now in their seventies, still live in their beloved Streatham.

Alan Weeks, presenter of Pot Black, and Ted Lowe prepare for another session.

THE continuation of a high standard of Pot Black has been guaranteed by the introduction of Junior Pot Black in 1981. Although some people are apprehensive that too much snooker is appearing on television and think we risk over-exposure by presenting the kids, I believe it to be essential to show junior snooker on TV and do not consider that it conflicts with the professionals.

Pot Black did more to resurrect snooker than anything else. We set out to discover new faces at the risk of upsetting more established players—and it has worked. One case of opportunity knocking was that of Graham Miles in 1974. He was included as a reserve but when Fred Davis withdrew due to illness, Miles stepped in, won the tournament and set up the highest break—and, to show it wasn't a fluke, Graham won again the following year.

To keep Pot Black always high in the television ratings, it is essential to infuse fresh talent. It was the problem of too few names and not enough new faces that caused the game to slump earlier. Junior Pot Black is the breeding ground for the stars of the 1990s. It gives youngsters the chance to develop natural talent and increase their confidence. Even some mature players could not produce their best form when they first appeared under TV lights and in front of the cameras. It can be an ordeal for a shy lad to have to appear on television, but if introduced to it early on, it should not come as a shock when he is a little older. Already Junior Pot Black has a TV audience of millions.

A series featuring up-and-coming youngsters had been suggested to the BBC two or three years earlier. The event that really convinced the bosses to give the go-ahead to Reg Perrin's idea was the emergence of Steve Davis, who made his Pot Black debut in 1979 and caught the eye of millions to show that snooker had now become a young man's sport—and one that fascinated women viewers. By the time Junior Pot Black appeared for the first time in May 1981, Davis had become world champion.

The BBC started the ball rolling in 1980, inviting through the *Radio Times* boys up to nineteen to send in their qualifications for possible inclusion in the proposed series. More than two hundred applications were received from lads of nine upwards. With the help of the Billiards and Snooker Control Council, the letters were sorted out and a short list was eventually reduced to twelve competitors. The first Junior Pot Black champion was Dean Reynolds, from Grimsby, and to prove it was a merited win, the eighteen-year-old Dean went on to take the British Junior championship. His early success was almost certainly due to the fact that at sixteen, within six months of leaving school to work, he was made redundant. So, with little other choice, he decided to become a full-time professional snooker player after his first success in Junior Pot Black.

Dean Reynolds had taken up the game when twelve. At fifteen he joined the Garth Snooker Club at Grimsby. That first job had been as a trainee motor mechanic and inevitably he was among the first to be laid off when jobs became scarce. He spent hours practising and was rewarded by becoming Lincolnshire junior champion for two years. Dean, a left-hander, still practises four or five hours each day and claims to have already made a maximum 147 break in 1980 and many century breaks. At nineteen he turned

Dean Reynolds, first winner of Junior Pot Black in 1981.

professional and convinced some experts that he has a big future when he made his first appearance in the world championships in 1982.

A youngster who has impressed me very much is John Parrott from Liverpool. Standing over six feet, John seemed so confident when he appeared in Junior Pot Black when he was eighteen. Though he finished runner-up to Dean Reynolds, he walked off with the highest break prize of 98. He won the Junior Pot Black 1982 title, having already taken the North-West junior championship and appeared in the Northern and the British Under-19 championship finals. His greatest claim to fame was in the final of the 1982 Pontin's Open when he defeated Ray Reardon. In a practice game against a club member at the Golden Leisure

Snooker Centre, Parrott made his highest break to date. The young Irish star Paddy Browne, unable to play in 1983, allowed John Parrott back as a late invitation—he took the title for the second year running.

Though only eighteen and still an amateur John was able to sign a contract endorsing a range of cues, worth around £5,000 to him. The position of an amateur at snooker is strange. Since 1972 amateurs have been allowed to accept prize money and exhibition fees. John, for instance, won £2,000 when he beat Reardon at Prestatyn. But as the International Billiards and Snooker Federation, which controls world amateur champions, does not

John Parrott, Junior Pot Black Winner 1982 and 1983. Is he a world champion of tomorrow?

allow amateurs to endorse snooker equipment, Parrott is now ineligible for the world amateur championships. Yet the Billiards and Snooker Control Council, the world governing body of the game both professional and amateur, has no ban on amateurs endorsing snooker equipment. It is all very complicated, but doesn't bother John Parrott. He is now a professional and I am sure you will be seeing a lot of him in the future.

There are plenty of other kids I have watched who convince me that there is much talent queuing up to become the stars of the 1990s—boys like Steve Ventham, from Mitcham, who made his Junior Pot Black debut when only sixteen in 1982 and reaching the semi-final before losing to the accomplished Parrott. Others who caught my eye were Paddy Browne, from Dublin, the All-Ireland junior and senior champion; Chris Hamson, Mark Lockwood, John Keers, the fourteen-year-old Stephen Hendry and several others.

Obviously, boys of sixteen or seventeen show more nerves than the professionals, but it is a pleasure to see how these lads, having got over stage fright, settle down and play like veterans. The sad thing is when a boy gets knocked out before he has settled down, and does not get another game. This, of course, is the criticism of the 'sudden death' policy that the professionals have against Pot Black, but it is great experience for the juniors and part of growing up and becoming a good pro.

CHAPTER 3

TV – The Big Break

THERE can be no doubt that the television boom snooker is enjoying today dates back to the instant success of Pot Black 69. There are now many more sponsors, far more lucrative prizes and advertising contracts, but the revolution from the depression of the 1950s and 1960s came about in that old cinema in Birmingham when many professionals were sceptical about a recorded snooker programme in which the best-named players of the day risked humiliation on the result of one frame. The world championship itself came back from the dead. John Pulman had remained champion from 1964 to 68. But in 1969 these championships reverted to an open tournament.

Such was the success of the first Pot Black series that BBC and ITV producers called conferences and formed research groups to examine the new television phenomenon. Viewing

Steve Davis and Ray Reardon pose for the photographer before a big tournament while referee John Williams talks to Eddie Charlton and Ted Lowe.

charts and ratings were beginning to be turned upside down and the Cinderella game was to rock soccer, boxing, wrestling, show jumping and other big sports. Eventually TV snooker was to compete in the ratings against some of the most popular non-sporting series that had been running for years.

Big companies, especially tobacco and beer groups, looking to sponsor sport but ignoring snooker as one of yesterday's games, suddenly sat up and took notice, as did the advertising agents and public relations firms, now all hustling to get on the gravy-train. What surprised them all most was that women too had become compulsive viewers. Now the advertisers were dealing with a new audience exceeding five million and growing all the time.

The popularity of snooker among women viewers takes some explaining. One of the reasons for it must be that their image of middle-aged men pottering around a table was so wildly wrong! And the individual charm of the players, as well as the fascination of their snooker skills, may well have something to do with it as well. The series format of Pot Black lets viewers get to know the players and identify with them a bit like characters in a popular serial or soap opera, while the intimacy and immediacy of the 'sudden death' contest is emotionally and dramatically appealing. Whether you are nailbiting with the Hurricane or admiring Steve Davis's composure, it all adds up to more than a game—sheer magical excitement as the youngsters, the mature champions and the rebels wrap themselves round the table. Everybody has their favourite player, and both men and women can enjoy snooker on different levels; in the end, of course, the 'vital statistics' that count are the ones that appear on the scoreboard.

With ITV chasing the BBC in a ratings duel, the eruption of prize money and audiences in less than a decade has indeed been revolutionary. Whereas at Leicester Square we were grateful if a newspaper put up £1,000 or £1,500 in prizes, tobacco companies together with household manufacturers were moving in and if they were a little cautious at the start, they were soon to make successful snooker players among the richest of sportsmen. Player's No. 6, for instance, put up £3,500 for the 1969 world championships. There were only eight entries and the winner, John Spencer, collected £1,300—a big proportion of the total cash. By 1983 Embassy Cigarettes were putting up £135,000 for the championships and seventy-four competitors were chasing the first prize of £30,000.

The 1969 championships were the start of something big but were still organized round the country in centres like Bolton, Stratford, Southampton and Stoke; however, they heralded the end of an era when John Spencer beat John Pulman in the first round and went on to become champion for the first time, beating Gary Owen in the final at the Victoria Hall, London.

The world championships were held twice in 1970. In the spring, sponsored again by Player's No. 6, eight competed at Grimsby and Bolton and Reardon became champion for the first time, beating Pulman in London. This was John's last appearance in a world championship final and Ray's first of six victories. In the autumn of the same year the championships were staged in Australia for the first time with nine entries. Eddie Charlton organized it all without an outside sponsor and John Spencer was pleased to collect £2,333, nearly double what Reardon had received in London, when beating Warren Simpson.

The championships final did not take place in 1971. Player's No. 6 lost interest in the event and the 1971 championships were spread round the country with the final staged in London in February 1972. Though sixteen took part, it was sponsored with individual promoters negotiating the prize money. In his first attempt Alex Higgins became the first qualifier to go on to become world champion, beating Spencer and very happy to collect £480.

Park Drive were the next tobacco firm to take interest. Alex Higgins had become a box-office name with a massive TV audience. Park Drive had already sponsored three £2,000 tournaments in 1971 and 1972 and decided to put up £8,000 for the 1973 world championships. We all felt that the 1972 championships had dragged on far too long and did not have the impact of Pot Black, and that they should be streamlined. So the whole event was staged at the City Exhibition Halls in Manchester over two weeks, on the lines of the Wimbledon tennis championships. Entries had risen to twenty-three. Up to this time the BBC had shown more interest in televising Pot Black than the world championships. Now they decided to cover the later stages for the first time. The event was successful. Ladbroke's set up a betting office inside the building and much publicity was given to Reardon's 38-32 victory over Charlton.

Park Drive took the 1974 tournament to the King's Hall, Belle Vue, Manchester, but it was too big an arena for snooker and with Reardon easily beating Graham Miles in a disappointing final, Park Drive lost interest. Without a sponsor anxious to step in, Eddie Charlton applied to stage the championships in Australia again, and in an exciting final Ray beat Eddie, 31-30.

By 1976 Embassy Cigarettes had taken the event over, pouring £15,000 into it. The early games took part at Middlesbrough Town Hall with the final stages at the Wythenshaw Forum in Manchester. It was yet another Reardon year with Ray taking good care of Higgins, 27-16. The sponsors were not all that happy and it was not certain that they would carry on in 1977, but Mike Watterson, a player and new promoter, had some bright ideas which appealed to Embassy. He was prepared to take a gamble and booked the Crucible Theatre in Sheffield at his own expense. The prize money was increased to £17,000. It was the finest thing to happen to the championships since the days of Leicester Square and, of course, it was now a much bigger event. The Crucible, an attractive and modern building, was perfect in every way for big snooker. BBC producer Nick Hunter became very enthusiastic and persuaded his bosses into increased television coverage. Apart from the TV interest, more than 20,000 people paid to watch the games over a fortnight. John Spencer won his third world title—and this time the prize had gone up to £6,000. The runner-up was Cliff Thorburn. Cliff played with a two-piece cue, always very popular in Canada; when he reached the world title final for the first time, it caused a boom in Canada.

These were the most successful championships yet staged and snooker was going from

Jack Karnehm, the B.S.C.C. national coach for billiards and snooker, became a TV commentator in 1978, and has already had the luck to cover two maximum breaks. Here he joins Ted Lowe for the first time to cover the world championships for that year.

strength to strength. There was no doubt of the popularity of staging the whole event under one roof in a two-week period. In 1978, a delighted Embassy increased their cash to £24,000, with £7,500 first prize. A record twenty-eight players took part and for the first time Nick Hunter gave daily coverage with five million viewers watching most of the time and seven million glued to the box for the final, which saw Reardon taking his sixth title, plus more international interest as South African Perrie Mans reached his first final. Sadly, I shall never forget the 1978 championships. Poor Joe Davis collapsed during the semi-final between his brother Fred and Mans. It had been a tense match and too much for Joe's suspect heart. The old maestro never got his health back 100% again.

Reardon's sixth world title victory signalled the end of another period in which one man dominated the championships. Now more and more young players were arriving on the scene, having been encouraged and inspired after watching the Spencers and Reardons on television. They were hungry and ambitious challengers. In 1979 a quiet Welshman, Terry

Griffiths, who had been a postman and insurance agent, became world champion at his first attempt and picked up the now worthwhile first prize of £10,000. The Welshman was hailed as a new super player but even Terry could not repeat his win the following year when Cliff Thorburn, improving on his runner-up's achievement of three years earlier, became Canada's first world champion with victory in a dour final against Higgins. There was no halting the progress of snooker and the game snatched an even bigger viewing public and more headlines in the national press in 1981 when Steve Davis, the auburn-haired lad from Plumstead who had been knocking at the door since he was twenty-one, came through and won the world title at twenty-four, beating Welshman Doug Mountjoy. That year Davis won every major tournament. His very name lent itself to publicity. Joe had been Mister Snooker for most of his life and Fred had done remarkably well after Joe retired. Now arrived another Davis, unrelated, but so talented that the Press rather prematurely began to forecast that the new Davis would dominate the game for years and might be greater than the original king because Steve was playing amid fiercer competition and under greater pressure.

Steve, unlike Joe, already had a powerful agent behind him before he became world champion. In Barry Hearn, he not only had an agent, but an accountant, a tycoon of snooker halls and a good friend. Hearn declared openly that Davis was something special and would become a millionaire before he was thirty.

That final between Steve Davis and Doug Mountjoy had created so much interest because of the younger man's build-up that it is estimated that 16 million viewers saw it, though it went on until after midnight. Yet even Davis, with so much talent and so much ballyhoo behind him, could not retain his title. In 1982 he not only went the way of every defending champion since Spencer won in 1977 by failing to hold the title, but was unbelievably slammed 10-1 in the first round by Bolton's Tony Knowles. The eventual winner was Alex Higgins, making a tremendous and emotional comeback by beating Reardon, and picking up £25,000 compared with the £480 he had collected for his only previous victory ten years earlier. (This figure alone illustrates how the game had emerged from being almost a minor sport to the richest.) The extraordinary Irishman had to claw back from behind, and we had the usual mixture of nail-biting, agitated smoking—plus tears when the Hurricane insisted that his wife bring his baby daughter in full view of the cameras after he had won.

What extraordinary television entertainment this added up to. There were thrills for the genuine snooker fans and all the public tears and emotion in the style of *This is Your Life* that please many viewers. The BBC had filmed 144 hours of play and condensed it into seventy hours, and the audience was nearly ten times the size of the original Pot Black audience of 1969. A few months after the 1982 championships Tony Knowles, who had become a TV star without having won a major tournament by his massacre of Davis, attracted a big audience when he captured his first big prize, beating David Taylor in the final of the Jameson International Open. For this, the Bolton player received £23,000 plus £2,500 for the highest break. The television snooker revolution had transformed snooker players from enthusiastic sportsmen like Joe Davis into business tycoons. While one wishes them well, inevitably—like the soccer player of the 1960s—snooker players are now in danger of becoming slaves to greed. The old players earned small money but did not have the same pressures. There was a lot more fun in the game, but I suppose, in fairness, had the old players had the same opportunity to become tycoons they would have rushed to join the rat-race too.

I AM often asked why I developed my softly, softly approach to commentating. Did I work on it or did it just happen naturally? The answer is simple. The hushed commentaries were born at Leicester Square Hall when the BBC began televising. I had long given up playing in serious amateur competition to become one of Britain's first 'Grade A' referees along with Bruce Donkin. The top sports commentator in those days was Raymond Glendenning of the famed handlebar moustachio. Because of my knowledge of the game both as player and referee, the BBC arranged for me to sit immediately behind Raymond

(Below) Whispering Ted in one of his earliest BBC broadcasts from Bristol; an obliging colleague takes precautions against Ted developing a dry throat. In 1947 *(top right)* the BBC set up the equipment for an early television broadcast in the basement at Leicester Square Hall: producer Michael Henderson explains technicalities to Walter Donaldson and John Barrie. And an up-to-date Ted *(below right)* takes up his position behind the camera.

1
BBC tv
colour
COURIER
RULES
O.K.

and guide him on the technicalities of the game. Glendenning had a superb rich voice and was a tremendous pro but at times was more of an entertainer than an accurate commentator, and while this could, and still does, go on with radio commentaries, the television reporter is talking about events that the public is actually watching.

There was no commentary box at the Leicester Square Hall and Glendenning could not talk too loudly for fear of interrupting the players in action; I virtually had to scribble notes or whisper because I was only keeping him on the right lines and my voice was not to be heard on the air.

One day Glendenning lost his voice and the BBC asked me to stand in for him. The microphone was less than six feet away from the billiards table and I was almost as close to play as a boxing commentator at the ringside. In the case of boxing, the crowd roar so much that there is never any fear of a contestant hearing a radio or TV voice; but with snooker there is, of course, a complete hush as the player prepares to take his shot and, being manager of the hall and a referee, I was even more conscious that I must not disturb the players and I literally whispered the whole broadcast.

I continued the soft approach with my early TV commentaries. There were mixed reactions. In 1958 I had a friendly letter from Douglas Fleming of the BBC after one of my performances. It was the first time I had operated from inside a commentary box and I still whispered. He gave me some encouragement by saying he thought I had coped very well with the 'to-ings' and 'fro-ings' of the afternoon and I improved as I went along. Then he added:

> There seem to be two schools of thought about the situation. It appears that some people like the whispered commentary because they feel it's part of the atmosphere. I don't myself go quite as far as this, and I think we have probably found the right compromise in putting you in the box; (a) I think it gives you more confidence, and (b) because you are still in the position to use very much more voice. For my money, therefore, this is the right answer, and one that I could repeat.

I was most grateful for the help and advice and as time went by, the consensus of opinion favoured the soft approach. By the time I was first asked to work out a formula for Pot Black and be the commentator I had had much experience and the producer was particularly interested that I should continue with my whispering performance. Commentating isn't as simple as it sounds. You can't rehearse before the event, but you must do your homework, researching into facts about the players.

As the viewers only hear my voice and don't see me, I hasten to explain that sometimes one needs eyes in the back of one's head. The box in the Birmingham studio where Pot Black is recorded is erected over the black spot, twenty feet up. There is a black and white monitor, a colour monitor and ear-phones through which I listen to both producer and director of the programme. And I also take a look out of the box to get a general view of the game. It could be an ordeal for a complete newcomer gazing first at one monitor, then the other and at the same time having to listen to directions through the earphones. I must not, of course, reply to any instructions directed at me as this would be heard by the viewers. My conversation with the director or producer is done over a private link known as the 'lazy' microphone.

It is my policy to talk as little as possible. My job is to remain unobtrusive and simply help the viewer understand and enjoy the game. In the early days of TV it was necessary to explain shots and even the value of the colours but today viewers are knowledgeable and would not want me to explain that a certain player is about to put the blue in the middle pocket when it is obvious. It's a question of timing which comes with experience and knowing when and when not to speak. Sometimes silence is golden.

Naturally, producers and directors have to cut out many incidents unless the programme is live. So it's no good my chatting away if I sense that a certain happening, such as a player taking too much time preparing his shot, is likely to be cut. On the other hand, I must not underestimate the use of words. There are occasions when you just have to say something because there will always be a small percentage of viewers out of the millions who still don't really understand the game and expect to be told details with which the majority of fans are already familiar.

Say, for instance, the director instructs the cameraman to focus on a player's bridgehand and I happen to be looking out from my box, seeing the possibilities open to the player, but overlook the fact that the camera is on his bridgehand; then the director will quietly prompt me. Or the producer may see somebody in the audience he would like me to mention. All this makes up the package of the programme. But neither producer nor director can be expected to read what is going on in the mind of a player. This is where my experience and knowledge of the game comes in and is the reason for our summarists, John Spencer and Rex Williams. We give a broad hint to the backroom boys by weighing up the possibilities of the next shot so that the camera is ready. It is easy to be caught out. Once, when Steve Davis was in action, the green ball was over the centre pocket, very acute, with the rest of the colours sitting pretty. I felt sure Steve would attempt to cut the green into the centre pocket and the cameras were prepared. Instead, Davis promptly slammed the green straight up the table into the top pocket. It went like a rocket and was a brilliant shot but as cameramen can't move faster than sound, the shot was missed. I was caught out but whispered calmly: 'Davis has fooled me. It was a brilliant shot'. Everybody was happy.

One thing that is vital during the four-day recording of Pot Black between Christmas and the New Year is the complete security of the results of the matches to be shown later. It is absolutely sacrosanct that nobody connected with the programme divulges a result. Many a time a snooker fan has tried to persuade me to tell them in confidence the Pot Black winner. I become both deaf and dumb. The integrity of Pot Black is that a winner has never yet been disclosed. If there were a leak, imagine how a betting coup could be brought off.

Though I realise my voice is now recognised by millions, both in the United Kingdom and in Australia, I am visually anonymous and am, therefore, unrecognised by the masses when I walk about London, Manchester, Glasgow and Birmingham. And that's how I like it. I accept that my voice, and not my face, is my fortune. I like being one of the backroom boys of snooker.

I have been happy to stay with my favourite sport though I did once cover the World's bowls championships. I like to listen to the expert on his subject. There is only one Dan Maskell or Peter O'Sullevan. There was only one John Arlott. I like to think there is only one Ted Lowe. However, there has been the odd occasion when I strayed from snooker. During that very severe winter of 1963 the ice and snow interrupted our soccer, racing and most outdoor sports for many weeks. I had already recorded a series on snooker for the BBC and being a freelance at that time I had also contracted a snooker assignment for ITV from the National Liberal Club in London.

Due to the interruption of soccer, the Pools Association decided for the first time to form a panel of experts to forecast what the results would have been had they been played in order to keep the customers filling in their coupons. I was invited by Denis Monger, a good friend and one of the stalwarts of BBC outside broadcasting, to introduce the panel and to announce their decisions. I accepted because I did not require any special knowledge of football but little did I realise the panel would sit for so many weeks. All of us were locked in the Exhibition Room of the Connaught Rooms in London and the security was such that special locks were put on the doors and individual keys handed to each of us. The Pools people were afraid of some villain trying to get at one of the panel and though nothing happened I now realise what life must be like at Fort Knox.

I rather enjoyed my spell, meeting personalities like Sir Gerald Nabarro, A. P. Herbert and Sir Douglas Bader, Arthur Ellis, the well-known referee, George Young, Scotland's international, one of my England heroes, Tommy Lawton, and several other stars. But I had a big problem building up. Thank goodness my son Michael was with me. Apart from having to dash in taxis between the Connaught Rooms and Whitehall, I was embarrassed by the clash of my commentaries. One Saturday afternoon became Ted Lowe's benefit. I was seen on ITV covering snooker. If you switched over to BBC, you would also find me on snooker. In between this I was reading out the Pools Panel football results on BBC1 and 2 for radio. In all, I could be seen or heard on five TV and radio programmes at the same time! My son—oh, yes, he found all the taxis for me.

The early days of television commentary had their problems. Apart from not having a box, there was also a lack of link men. I would have to hand over directly to Charlie Staircase at the speedway track or Bill Snooks at the boxing ringside. It could be difficult on occasions. There were also times when a sports commentator had to make a special announcement in no way connected with the event he was covering. Once I had a delightful announcement to make during a snooker tournament in February 1964, when my producer calmly interrupted me to say: 'I want you to make an announcement in your own good time, Ted, during the next five or ten minutes that Princess Alexandra has just delivered her first child—a son'. The subject of royalty reminds me of one of the most memorable moments of my life and it has nothing to do with snooker. During my job with Allied Breweries I had to call at the most interesting places—it could be a four-ale bar, a billiards room in a club, a West End hotel or a staff party at Clarence House. I twice had the honour of attending the staff Christmas parties at Clarence House and on each occasion dancing with that gracious lady the Queen Mother.

One of my toughest broadcasts was at the world championship final in 1950 at the Tower Circus, Blackpool. Not only was there no commentary box but never before or since have I sat so far away from a billiards table to do a commentary. I never want it to happen that way again. I was perched on a seat well up in the gods looking down on the circus ring. Below me were two tiny dots battling for the world title. They were Fred Davis and Walter Donaldson. It was as much as I could do to see the colours and it would have been a

Ted Lowe introduces the first ever Soccer Pools Panel during the postponed matches in 1963. Sir Gerald Nabarro was the chairman on this occasion.

terrible ordeal for a commentator not steeped in the game. I was grateful that I had been a player since the age of seven, a referee in my twenties and didn't need any help from outside.

I had another strange experience of this kind. Joe Davis and Jack Rea, the Irishman with the Charlie Chaplin walk, were playing at the Rusholme Conservative Club, Manchester. The microphone was erected in the seat where the drummer in the local dance band sat! I squeezed in between the drums, piano and monitor and was far from happy. Again I was glad I knew the game backwards, otherwise the commentary could have been disastrous.

I pride myself I know how to keep my cool. If I didn't I might have panicked and blown my top up in the gods at Blackpool or jammed in the drummer's seat at Rusholme Conservative Club. Only once did I ever noticeably raise my voice. This was in a match between the Irishmen Alex Higgins and Patsy Fagan. The Hurricane had to play a long, slow agonizing shot to get at the pink, which wobbled in the jaws of the pocket and didn't go down. 'He's missed it!' I shouted. It let in Fagan who took the frame. I had my leg pulled for weeks after this incident and was temporarily nicknamed 'Screeching Ted!'

It was the only time in many years I forgot to keep the brakes on, though deep down inside I have been very excited at some of the great matches I have seen. Part of my experience is to anticipate every shot a player will make, but I got nicely 'caught and bowled' once by my old friend John Pulman. It was during the early days of televised snooker when it was part of my job to predict nearly every shot so as to educate a big new audience with many viewers who did not understand the game. Pulman was at the table and I was explaining to folk at home the finesse of positional play and the build-up of a big break. I was in full flow: 'Pulman', I said with confidence, 'is now about to take the red and will come off the side cushion to position himself on the black'. John obliged perfectly. I continued: 'Following this black, Pulman will go down the table for the red just at the top of the pack and will be well placed for the black again'. Once more Pulman did his stuff. I continued happily for another five or six shots, forecasting with great accuracy every move Pulman made, when quite unexpectedly he ran out of position. Pulman turned to me where I was sitting some four feet from the table with no box and, imitating my voice, whispered: 'Ted. Do you mind if I play my own bloody game now!' At least he had a twinkle in his eyes . . .

Another time I was caught with my trousers down but was completely unaware of what I had said. Fred Davis was preparing to play a shot from a difficult position. He put his leg on the table in an endeavour to reach the cue ball. After toying with using the rest he decided to play the shot with his left hand and was successful. While he was making up his mind I had said innocently in hushed tones: 'Fred Davis, the doyen of snooker, now sixty-seven years of age and too old to get his leg over, prefers to use his left hand'.

I heard the laughter from my producer and engineers in the earphones but still didn't know why until later when I asked what it was all about. It took me a long time to live that one down with the TV crew and I've heard some of the professionals who give a display of trick shots at the end of an exhibition use this very story as part of their patter.

One other boob I was not allowed to forget was made during a Pro-Celebrity tournament at Leeds when I came out with: 'And for those of you watching this in black and white, the pink sits behind the yellow'. Again I didn't realise what I had said until I was told later. But at least I made *The Times* under the heading: 'The Potty Quote of the Week'. More recently during the opening frame of a championship a red and colour had been taken before I uttered a word. My opening line—'The first balls of the championship'.

Private Eye, the satirical magazine, have a lot of fun with the clangers commentators drop and pay their readers a small fee for spotting those good enough to be published under the heading 'Colemanballs'. Over the years I've whispered a few such as:

> 'And Alex Higgins has literally come back from the dead'.
> 'One mistake here could win or lose the match either way'.
> 'Cliff Thorburn has been unsettled by the erratic but consistent potting of Perrie Mans'.
> 'It's not easy to get a snooker when there's only one ball on the table'.
> 'Perrie Mans played a prominent part in this tournament in 1979. In fact, he won it'.
> 'Higgins first entered these championships ten years ago. That was the first time, of course'.
> 'The audience are literally electrified and glued to their seats'.

Just to prove that I'm not the only broadcaster who raises a laugh, I'll pass on a few samples duly noted:

> 'Real possession of the ball this. And Zico's lost it!' John Helm
> 'And a sedentary seagull flies by'. Brian Johnstone
> 'Nick Holmes also got two today as Southampton won 3-0 at Leeds. Nick Holmes got the other'. Tony Gubba
> 'Two little jumps there. One big one and one small one'. David Vine
> 'There is Brendan Foster by himself with 2,000 people'. David Coleman
> 'Lawrenson slipped the ball through to Williams and he beat Shilton from 35 yards—and you don't beat Shilton from 35 yards'. Peter Jones
> 'Oh! That cross-court angle was so acute, it doesn't exist'. Dan Maskell
> 'It was like the Sixties, but it wasn't the Sixties. It was 1969'. Jimmy Savile

It all adds up to a bit of fun. If commentators can't join in with the rest of the world and laugh at themselves, they must cry alone. Mark you, it is always easy to spot the other man's mistake, especially when you've never tried commentating yourself. Everybody laughs when somebody slips on a banana skin—everybody except the person who slips.

CHAPTER 4

Snooker Room Stories

IN MORE than thirty years' broadcasting I can't recall a more dramatic interruption than during the 1980 Embassy world championship final between Cliff Thorburn and Alex Higgins. The match itself was as tense as one could expect to see with Higgins smoking cigarette after cigarette, when viewers sitting at home suddenly saw flashed on their screens the bold SAS attack on the Iranian Embassy in Kensington, which had been under siege with many hostages held. The Hurricane looked so worried and drained that people in their homes must have thought Alex and Cliff knew what was going on in Kensington but they didn't have a clue. Neither did the large audience sitting in the Crucible Theatre at Sheffield. While spectators became more tense as the game reached a critical stage, the viewers suddenly saw the flash and heard the explosion of bombs going off as the SAS men went into the Embassy.

I always have two monitors, one showing the picture of the action in front of me and the other of the picture being sent to the public at large. So I was able to keep one eye on what was going on at the Iranian Embassy while making sure I didn't get caught out if viewers were switched back to Sheffield. Through the ear phones I was wearing for comments from my producer and director I could hear all the other instructions to cameramen and floor manager—you have to get used to the continual talk and make sure it does not interfere with your own concentration. The commentator learns to shut out remarks that are not directed at him personally. In the final session I was fully engrossed in Alex Higgins's efforts to overcome the much slower Canadian when suddenly my producer shouted: 'Ted! Stop talking at the end of this sentence!' Instinctively, I was silent and after what seemed ages but was only a matter of seconds, I heard a loud bang through the earphones. The SAS had gone into action.

Understandably, the television and radio lines were in a turmoil. Conversations were going back and forth as to how long both TV and radio would stay covering the siege when again suddenly my producer warned me: 'Ted! They are coming back to you *now!*' So as if we were just resuming after an interval I whispered: 'And so from one Embassy we return you to this Embassy—world snooker final . . .'

All the time, oblivious to the excitement, Thorburn, quietly, and Higgins, agitatedly, continued the tense battle in front of a big crowd, unaware that millions of TV viewers at home had seen a film that will remain forever in the memories of those who watched it. Perhaps nothing demonstrates the popularity of snooker more tellingly than the fact that we received complaints that the championship broadcast had been interrupted.

That was one of the most tense commentaries of my thirty years in the broadcasting business. However, in half a century with the game as boy and man, I've had much fun and many laughs. I would have to admit there was more fun in my days at Leicester Square because there was less at stake than today when the prizes have become so enormous that I do not believe any professional plays any more for fun. When Bill Shankly, the late and great manager of Liverpool Football Club, was asked if he considered football on Merseyside to be a matter of life and death, he replied: 'It's more important than that!' And that's how the ambitious professionals approach snooker today.

In the more relaxed days we could all afford to let our hair down and I had some happy occasions with Joe Davis and later with John Pulman. A small band of us used to drop into the Greyhound pub in Kensington some evenings. The pub was round the corner from where Joe Davis lived and was run by a snooker addict and great character named Johnny Caulfield. Johnny ran regular tournaments at the Greyhound and I twice reached the finals. Many personalities like Sir Gordon Richards, Len Harvey, the heavyweight champion, Sid Field, Jack Warner, Sid James and others frequented the pub because there was always a laugh to be shared. Inevitably, we sometimes stayed after closing time as the guests of Mine Host. One evening Johnny had invited a dozen of us to remain. Around one o'clock in the morning a jolly, corpulent, middle-aged man, about to fall asleep, decided he must go. The 'Guv'nor' let him out the door and Joe Davis, John Pulman, myself and a few others continued telling stories until nearly an hour later there was some hefty banging at the front door. Johnny opened it cautiously to see our little fat friend, gently swaying with an overcoat over his pyjamas: 'Where's my wife?' he demanded. 'I got to bed and she isn't there. I think I left her in the billiards room'.

And there in the snooker room we found the dear lady, fast asleep on a bench settee.

John Pulman and I had a wonderful outing to Dublin after I had joined Allied Breweries. One of my directors wanted me to go to Ireland on business and thought it a good idea for me to invite a professional player to go along so that we could throw in a few exhibitions for the barmen of Dublin. A hall had already been hired. I asked John if he would like to accompany me and he readily agreed. We turned it into a relaxed trip and took the boat from Holyhead to Dun Laoghaire where we were met and taken to our hotel by car. John and I enjoyed reminiscing most of the night and joined in a few drinks with some jovial Irishmen. We were fairly tired by the time the boat docked. So much so, that we told our generous hosts that we would skip breakfast and go straight to our rooms and get our heads down for a few hours to be fresh for the exhibition match that evening. We were a little concerned when we were told a lunch had already been arranged and our hosts would pick us up at noon.

We collected our room keys from the receptionist. John was in Room 26 and I was in Room 28, so I inquired a little facetiously who was in Room 27 'Room 27 is especially set up for a few drinks for Mr Pulman and yourself, sir', I was informed by an attractive colleen with smiling Irish eyes. That was the understatement of the year! Room 27 had been turned into the biggest bar I ever saw set up for two people. Every kind of drink ever brewed or distilled was there—and, of course, there were connecting doors from Rooms 26 and 28.

John and I agreed sleep was more important than drink and got to bed for a couple of hours, only to be awakened by the early arrival of our hosts who wanted to show us Dublin before lunch. In all my years in a business which thrived on entertaining and hospitality I had never before or since been the victim of more generous hosts. The lunch began with aperitifs around 12.30 and ended with liqueurs around 5.30. It was certainly a lunch to remember but it wasn't exactly perfect preparation for giving an exhibition of one's skills on a billiards table and I would say neither John nor I were our sharpest when we entered the hall packed with 400 Dublin barmen. The schedule was for John to take on six local amateurs and I would commentate. I was glad I didn't have to play! Pulman certainly wasn't seeing the ball as he should; he missed some easy shots and was beaten in his first three frames. We could hear the mutterings from the audience and realised the exhibi-

Famous actor, scriptwriter and comedian Eric Sykes was one of the original Pro-Celebrity snooker guests.

tion wasn't going down too well. I called an interval and made sure we got at the black coffee. We both agreed something must be done. Fifteen minutes later, we resumed and Pulman sank everything, overwhelming his next three opponents. John was determined to safeguard his reputation and hit the balls much harder than was necessary. The Dubliners were impressed as reds and colours were sent crashing into the pockets.

The muttering stopped and there was a cathedral-like hush as John built up a big break only to be shattered by a broad Irish brogue from the back gasping: 'It's fan******tastic!' The whole crowd burst out laughing at the choice adjective and John Pulman and myself were doubled up. He had to interrupt his break for thirty seconds before he continued with his deadly potting. Everybody left the hall happy and I am sure those 400 Dublin barmen were convinced John had deliberately lost the first three frames as part of the act so as to show them how good he really was after the interval.

Another good laugh developed after I got together with my friend Tony Hart, of United Rum Merchants Ltd, the owners of Canadian Club Whisky, in 1975 to arrange the first Pro-Celebrity snooker series for Yorkshire Television. The celebrities were chosen by the TV companies while I invited the professionals. In one of the matches comedian Les Dawson was partnering one of the pros against Kenny Lynch and another player. Kenny hadn't been playing too well but after a long time he finally potted a red and turned his achievement into a comic act, strutting around the table, beating his chest. He was fooling so much that he hadn't noticed the black ball sitting over the centre pocket. When he saw how easy his next shot was, he studied it like a champion and kept going back to examine the cue ball as though he had a difficult shot ahead. As he bent down to take the shot all laughter had died down. But Les Dawson broke the silence calling out: 'I shouldn't pot that if I were you, Ken. It might be a relative!'

It brought the house down and nobody laughed more than Kenny.

BELIEVE it or not, but rain has actually stopped play. And I'm not talking about cricket. Rain stopped play in a snooker match—and at Manchester where many a losing Test Match has been saved when the heavens opened. It happened during a world championship in the 1970s between Fred Davis and Alex Higgins. During the game a rainstorm was raging outside; eventually the roof began to leak and rain dripped on to the table as Fred was about to take a shot. Fred, quick to take advantage of the situation, grabbed an umbrella from a spectator, opened it up and delighted the local Press photographer as he walked round the table while the referee searched for something to cover the cloth. Fred told me it was the second time it had happened to him, as apparently some years earlier a similar incident occurred in an exhibition game in an old hall on an old table when heavy rain built up in a false ceiling and chose to come through so suddenly that his shirt and waistcoat were drenched—but that wasn't the same as in a world championship match.

The unexpected seemed to happen to Fred of the cuddly figure. His well-known grin always added to such occasions. One night he was demonstrating his trick shots and miscued a white ball smack into the middle of a spectatator's pint of Guinness. Another time, while putting pressure on a 'jump' shot, the cue ball landed in the middle of a log fire!

Once at a small club in Blackpool, Fred was going through his usual routine which included his comment: 'This is the most difficult shot I have ever attempted. Last time I tried I ripped the cloth'. The onlookers duly laughed but the club secretary, new to his job, and without a great sense of humour, hurried forward and pleaded: 'Perhaps you shouldn't try that shot tonight, Mr Davis. We need the table for a club tournament tomorrow!'

Fred's sense of humour has been known to be mischievous. In the early days at Leicester Square, John Pulman was well known for his outbursts when things went wrong. One afternoon when opposing Fred, Pulman made a mess of what normally for him would be a simple shot and, believing he had left his opponent in position to make a big break, stormed through the swing doors into my office and criticised himself with a string of unprintable words. I remained silently tactful when the buzzer system on the scoreboard to my office, there to signal a player to return to the match room, sounded off before the angry John even had time to light a cigarette. It meant Davis had also failed to make a break so John hurried back to the sound of laughter from the spectators. The cue ball was tight behind the brown, completely snookering the returning player. Fred sat back in his chair grinning and the gentle laughter became a roar as he glanced at John's glowering face and called out: 'Fasten your seat belts!'

Fred's experience of rain stopping play reminds me that Rex Williams had a similar experience in South Africa. Rex was playing in an old club in Durban when a tropical storm caused the rain literally to gush through the roof and it flooded the table.

I have never been present when rain stopped play at snooker, but I can recall when rain stopped a BBC commentary at a bowls match and I have never been so grateful. It happened on one of those rare occasions when the BBC asked me to report on an event other than snooker. Against my better judgement—I have always maintained that an expert should stick to the sport he knows—I agreed to commentate on a bowls tournament at Mortlake Club, which belonged to Watneys Brewery. As I had become a director of Allied Breweries, big rivals, there was some consternation that I should be the commentator but over a chat in the boardroom the matter was settled amicably.

Then my problems really started. I was not familiar with bowls players so I arrived early and began to scribble out details for background on foolscap pieces of paper with a Biro. The programme was to be recorded and shown later. While we were in the clubhouse, it began to rain heavily. I gathered my notes and went outside only to discover that I was to be perched in a chair at one end of the rink. It was raining buckets and my producer kindly arranged for somebody to hold an umbrella over me, but I was in trouble. Have you ever tried to read unfamiliar notes made with a Biro when it's raining cats and dogs? If so, you'll understand my dilemma, but somebody up there liked me and to my great relief the rain was so heavy that it got into the camera lenses and the recording had to be postponed. The rain got me out of an embarrassing situation.

It was a different story the following year when I was asked to cover the 1972 world bowls championships at Worthing along with David Vine. We had a most ornate and comfortable commentary box at Beach House Park. This was the only time I left the snooker scene completely and the whole operation went off well. I made some wonderful friends among the bowling fraternity from many parts of the world. They have a pleasant custom of exchanging their country's badges and as I had since I was a child loved to collect badges to wear in the lapels of my jackets, I was delighted to get a badge from the sixteen teams competing. I still treasure them; they represent Australia, Fiji, Hong Kong, Israel, Malawi, New Guinea, USA, South Africa, New Zealand, Jersey, Guernsey, England, Ireland, Scotland, Wales and Canada.

DESPITE the good times I had at Leicester Square, I also had plenty of headaches and heartaches. In fact, the pressure of those seven years with a combination of working hard and playing hard caused a breakdown and I went into hospital and was ordered by my doctor to take a complete rest. I was dealing with champions and though the money was not big at the time, champions have egos and snooker has its share of Prima Donnas who have to be cajoled or, alternatively, put down. I had to be nice guy, tough guy and diplomat rolled into one. One of the top professionals of his day even sued me—and he was my old mate Horace Lindrum. All rather extraordinary when I tell you we were so close that he asked me to be the Best Man at his wedding. But I am glad to report that on the occasion of my legal battle with Horace, the Best Man won!

It was 1950 and I was still chasing sponsors to promote the game. Sidney Smith persuaded the *Sporting Record*, a new Fleet Street newspaper living on borrowed time, to put up some cash to back a Masters' tournament on the lines of the golf event. It was open to any player who had reached the final of the world championships in the previous ten years.

Good pals. Ted is Best Man to Horace Lindrum at the Australian's wedding to Joy White, a B.S.C.C. secretary, at St-Martin's-in-the-Fields on 5 July 1949.

George Chenier had gone back to Canada and Peter Mans had returned to South Africa, but Horace Lindrum had decided to remain in Britain. Horace qualified, having lost to Joe Davis in the 1946 final, and I needed all the international flavour I could gather. Horace had also reached the final in 1937, when Joe beat him. The handicappers in the Masters' tournament felt justified in deciding that the Australian should receive 23 points. They gave Sidney Smith 21 points and decided that Joe Davis, Fred Davis and Walter Donaldson should play off scratch. Horace's ego was badly wounded, and he blamed me, but instead of telling me outright he brooded over it. His resentment grew as he made up his mind that I was deliberately belittling him. He was, of course, wrong because I liked him personally, but he had not won the world title and in 1950 was not playing as well as the others.

I did not realise how badly Horace's pride had been dented and how angry he was until after the handicap had been printed in the programme and announced to the Press. It was only then that I received a telephone call from him informing me: 'I shall not be playing in the Masters'. I've never lost to Fred Davis level. I've beaten Walter Donaldson, receiving 13 points. I'm fed up with the way you run things and I intend retiring from tournament snooker'. He was adamant and would not listen to me. I was not only surprised but cross, getting this news so late in the day, as I felt sure that if Horace had told me earlier how he felt we might have compromised and at least reduced his handicap. So I had no alternative but to arrange for a special amendment to be slipped in the Masters' programme, informing spectators that we regretted that Mr Horace Lindrum had retired from competitive snooker and apologising for any misleading information in the Leicester Square Hall programme.

I also mentioned the facts to the *Evening News* snooker reporter who telephoned me for latest news on the tournament, and a big story appeared in the sports gossip column that Horace Lindrum had withdrawn from the Masters' and all competitive snooker and in future would only play in exhibition games. I announced that his place in the first match against Sidney Smith would be taken by Alec Brown. Imagine then my surprise and further annoyance when a letter was delivered next day by hand to Leicester Square from a solicitor's office, informing me that their client Mr Horace Lindrum had instructed them to issue a writ against me and the directors of the Leicester Square Hall, claiming damages for injurious falsehood unless I agreed to withdraw the printed slip in the programme and took every possible step to correct the false statements I had made, pay a reasonable sum to their client to compensate him for injury sustained, and pay the costs their client had been forced to incur. It was the first time I had been threatened with legal action and I was not amused.

I had only carried out Lindrum's instructions by withdrawing him from the Masters' and had no intention of meeting any of the four demands made in the solicitor's letter. I denied the charges and, after showing the letter to Joe Davis and Sidney Smith, directors of Leicester Square Hall, went to a solicitor, instructing him to inform Lindrum that there was nothing doing. In fact, I pointed out in the letter that Sidney Smith had visited their client at his home and discussed the question of Lindrum's withdrawal from the tournament. Mr Lindrum confirmed he was retiring from competitive snooker and told Sidney he had no objection to him reporting this in a snooker column he was at that time writing for the *Sporting Record,* the sponsors of the Masters'.

Needless to say, Horace Lindrum never proceeded with the writ and the row faded with the years. Joe, Sidney and myself were annoyed with his behaviour and Joe took it to heart, especially as Horace's mother, a volatile lady, referred many times to the way Horace had been belittled with our handicapping, and nearly twenty years passed before I was able to bring these two splendid fellows together again. I arranged a dinner party for Joe, Horace, myself and our wives. I was delighted that the evening went off well and the hatchet was well and truly buried because shortly afterwards Horace went back to Australia and never returned to Britain.

THOUGH dozens of professionals and many amateurs have scored the maximum 147 break, some of them very many times, only five players have achieved the maximum break officially recognised by the Billiards and Snooker Control Council, the world governing body. To obtain official recognition the maximum break must be achieved on a table with standard size pockets, in front of a paying audience, with a certified referee officiating and the rules of the B.S.C.C. strictly observed. The only players to have achieved 147 under these conditions are Joe Davis (1955), Rex Williams (1965), Steve Davis (1982), Cliff Thorburn (1983) and Kirk Stevens (1984). As this book goes to press, the perfect score is made by Kirk Stevens in the 1984 Benson & Hedges Masters at Wembley. Steve's was the first 147 on TV while Thorburn scored the first maximum break in the world championships. Let me remind you that it took Joe Davis twenty-seven years of striving after registering his first century break in 1928. Incidentally, Joe Davis never received a penny from the first ever maximum but Cliff Thorburn and Kirk Stevens each earned £10,000.

There have been so many claims of 147, especially from Canada, that while I will mention some, I don't intend to name the numerous players, both young and old, who claim the achievement, because they were either made on non-standard tables with generous size pockets, or with lighter balls, without sufficient witnesses or in exhibition or practice games when some of the reds had been lined up in between the colours to make the break easier. But it's never simple.

I believe Willie Thorne claims more 147 breaks than any other player and has around 30 to his name. He did it the first time when only twenty-one in Osborne's snooker hall in Leicester. Willie freely admits his achievements mostly took place in practice at his own Leicester club when he breaks up the reds. Cliff Thorburn had made nineteen of his maximum breaks in Canada prior to his tremendous achievement at Sheffield, and Willie Thorne will be the first to agree that doing it in the world championships, when sometimes it is more important to play safe, or win the frame with so much cash at stake, is a remarkable performance; and that goes for Kirk Stevens, too!

When snooker was first played in India, Britain or Australia it was more a game of tactics than potting, with priority given to positioning the balls to prevent an opponent scoring. The appetite for century breaks, record breaks and the elusive 147 did not really begin until the 1920s. There were more amateurs than professionals and the first big breaks came from men who played only for pleasure. If you study old records you will find a Mr E. Mayhew made 59 in 1905; Mr F. Garside scored 73 in 1909 and the first century seems to be credited to Mr G. Hargest with 112 in 1915. The professionals joined in when the renowned John Roberts Junior registered 73 in 1907 and Albert Cope 83 in 1913. An Australian, Frank Smith Junior, claimed to be the first professional to make a century break with 116 in Sydney in 1918.

But far more important than all the unofficial claims is the build-up over the years towards achieving the 147 with official recognition. Joe Davis was twenty-seven when he made his first century against Fred Pugh at Manchester. Oddly, the spectators had paid to see Joe and Fred in a billiards match but at Joe's own suggestion they played an exhibition of snooker to demonstrate the twenty-two ball game which was just beginning to catch on. But Joe's 101 was scored on a standard table with standard balls, in public and with an approved referee. He made several centuries earlier in practice games but this was his first accepted century; it was fitting that Joe should also be the first player to make a recognised 147 break over a quarter of a century later.

The chasing of century breaks in Britain began back in 1919 when Tom Newman, a billiards champion rather than snooker king, scored 86. This was accepted as a record until a few years later Joe Davis increased it to 96. A few more years went by and Tom regained the record with 97. Joe could never resist a challenge and bettered the record four times with 100 (1928), 101 (1929) and 105 (1930)—the first century break in the world championships. He made it 114 in 1933, followed by 132, but on this occasion the table was not considered standard. Joe's 114 was accepted as the record till 1936 when it was equalled by Horace Lindrum and broken by Sidney Smith, who potted every ball on the table to total 133. Joe took back the record with 135 in 1937. Lindrum's 141 and a similar score by Davis in South Africa did not receive official blessing, but Joe, striving one day to reach 147, took the record to 137 and 138 in 1938. Joe kept edging towards his target, scoring 140 and then 141. In 1949 George Chenier set up a new world record with 144. Three weeks later Davis beat it with 146 against Chenier. Joe scored another 146 in 1955 and finally achieved what had seemed the 'impossible dream' with his first 147 in the final weeks before Leicester Square Hall closed.

The first 147 break was claimed by E.J. 'Murt' O'Donaghue, of Australia, at Griffiths, New South Wales, on 26th September 1934. O'Donaghue had made breaks of 134 and 136 in 1928 and playing at Auckland, New Zealand, he made consecutive breaks of 130, 138 and 118, none of which were accepted by the governing body. But a certificate was presented to him after his 147 and was signed by 135 spectators who witnessed the break. 'Murt' proudly framed it and hung it in his club. It was a pity that O'Donaghue, who I still meet on my trips "Down Under" and Joe Davis did not meet in a championship match. If they had, I believe Joe would have achieved his 147 many years earlier.

Within weeks of the official Davis 147 break, Rex Williams, then only twenty-one, made a maximum break on his own table, playing against a friend, but it took Rex another ten years to become only the second player to have a 147 break officially recognised. Rex did it against Manuel Francisco, the South African amateur champion, at the Princes Hotel, Newlands, Capetown, on 22 December 1965. A further seventeen years passed before Steve Davis became only the third recognised holder of the 147 score. Steve's great moment was in Oldham in 1982. It was the first time the achievement was seen on TV.

I am sure a few readers of this book will write and tell me that the maximum break is 155, but I would never accept such a freak score. It can only be made possible by an opponent committing a foul and leaving a free ball, thus giving away eight points for the player to add to his own score, and I would not regard these extra points as part of a normal break. I have heard it rumoured that Alex Higgins has made 155 this way, but if it is so, it was not made in a match and has never been officially recorded.

IT IS astonishing how much snooker has been taped on film or videotape. Nowadays both the BBC and ITV have crews filming every frame of every major tournament, just in case—but there have been some nailbiting misses in the past!

From 1977 Nick Hunter has videotaped every shot in major tournaments with the intention of scoring another BBC 'first' by showing millions of viewers the first televised 147 break. It was also my ambition to be the commentator on such an occasion—but we were both disappointed, for it was Granada who were rewarded for their vigilance when Steve Davis obliged at the Oldham Civic Centre on 11 January 1982 in the Lada Classic. (I signed an exclusive contract with the BBC in 1977.)

The reason that both the BBC and ITV crews suddenly treated the screening of the first 147 break as a matter of life and death was due to the fact that John Spencer actually made the maximum break in the Holstein Lager tournament at Slough in 1978. But to John's great disappointment and ITV's utter frustration, the history-making event was missed because the camera crew were making a break of their own—a tea break! In fairness to the crew, they were badly in need of some relief from what had been a marathon concentration over four days, but while it is easy to be wise with hindsight, it must go down as snooker's miss of the century. As for poor John Spencer, he had a second disappointment when his achievement—unseen by millions—failed to get B.S.C.C. blessing after a thorough examination of the table. And the final irony came when Steve Davis's 147 became the first to be seen on television: John Spencer was Steve's opponent and spent that frame sitting down watching Davis win by 147-0! Incidentally, Steve, world champion at the time, was beaten by Terry Griffiths in the final and received only £3,000 runners-up prize. But the same month he signed a £300,000 contract with John Courage—not bad for a young man who is almost a teetotaller. It seems making 147 on television is worth a fortune.

While the BBC could afford to smile at ITV's gaffe, it also meant they must not get caught in a similar situation and at every tournament after this, producers from both channels would not allow anybody to relax for a split second. In fact in the world championships in the same year the BBC were so determined that they should not get caught that they used more film than in any other two weeks of sport, including the World Cup, Olympic Games and Wimbledon. Nine cameras were focussed on two tables. The crews worked 45 minutes on and 30 minutes off so that every man was sharp and would not lose concentration. Literally miles of film was used in case somebody scored 147.

In Birmingham in 1979, the finish of an unofficial 147 break by Ray Reardon was recorded, but only part of the break was picked up on the camera and it was only shown by the BBC on a Welsh programme. What the snooker producers were really seeking was a maximum break shown live from start to finish to a mass audience—and for that they had to wait until 1982. Oddly, the BBC produced the goods in both 1983 and 1984.

Talking of history-making events reminds me of an unfortunate incident that happened to Joe Davis in 1962. Joe appeared on television in the days before colour, following another of my drives to get snooker on the screen despite the bad patch it was going through. Joe was then sixty-one and had not played seriously for some years, and even his one good eye was beginning to give him trouble; but he was more than willing to have a go and the BBC agreed to pay £100. As commentator I received twenty guineas (£21). Imagine what today's top players would have to say about fees like this! The BBC recorded six snooker programmes at Gosta Green for Grandstand, to be shown for fifteen minutes each at later dates. This was the entire coverage of the game on TV for the whole of 1962.

Being a real pro and a perfectionist, Joe went into training and practised on his own table for hours each day. He was determined not to be a flop on television. What a remarkable man he was. He was to play against six different opponents and came up with the first century break on television—exactly 100—against John Pulman. Joe was delighted with his achievement and was assured that the break, which had been made in the first frame, had been taped and would go into the archives. He was promised a copy of the tape but when he requested it later, he was told that there had been a misunderstanding and his century had not been recorded. Joe was fed up and for weeks made a nuisance of himself by making phone calls and even personal visits to the BBC, insisting that he knew the event had been taped, but the film could not be found. Joe was never to know that years after he had died, the film was found in the archives by one of the bright TV backroom boys, Ron Gubba. Ron transferred it to videotape and it was shown during the 1982 world championships and has been seen several times since. Though it is in black and white and has dated, many young fans were astonished at the speed with which Joe moved round the table and the swiftness of his shots. In fact, Alex Higgins had nothing on him—and don't forget the old maestro was then sixty-one. I hope Old Joe knows that his TV effort was not after all in vain and that it will be seen by millions in future.

Ted with his wife Iris relaxing in the bar at his home at Cooden Beach, Sussex. On display are just a few of the hundreds of souvenirs collected on his snooker travels.

CHAPTER 5

The Champions

King Joe

JUST as Walter Lindrum was the greatest billiards player the world has seen, so Joe Davis was without parallel as the King of Snooker. There will be the usual arguments about this claim with so many splendid young players around today, facing more competition and pressure, but until the others prove it to be otherwise, the record of Joe Davis over more than three decades says it all. Joe always accepted a challenge and could produce century breaks or set up new records when under pressure. He would, in my opinion, have beaten the super-players of today. Though overshadowed at billiards by Walter Lindrum, Joe still held the world billiards championship for five years between 1928 and 1932, the United

(Right) Walter Lindrum, the greatest billiards player of all time. And *(below)* it's 'Hello, Dolly' when Ted arrives in Melbourne: Walter's niece now runs the famous Lindrum Parlours.

Kingdom title for fourteen years between 1934 and 1947, and also the official world record break with 1,784.

Born at Whittington Moor, near Chesterfield, in 1901, Joe took up billiards before he was nine, playing in the room of his father's pub, the Queen's Hotel. Ernie Rudge, a Yorkshire professional, spotted the kid's outstanding talent and persuaded the father to allow Joe to be dolled up in an Eton collar and arranged for a local photographer to snap him. The boy was playing matches and giving exhibitions in pubs and clubs at fifteen shillings a time.

Joe scored his first 100 at billiards when only twelve, and in his teens could beat not only boys older than himself but many of the local amateurs and professionals. He won the junior professional title time after time and was so proficient at twenty that he went to London for the real championship and faced the highly respected Tom Newman. The well-established Newman showed Master Davis how to sort the men from the boys by handing out a severe trouncing.

But one of the qualities that made Joe a super champion was his determination to succeed; he also had fantastic dedication and pride. He went back to his Derbyshire village and practised more than ever, returning to Thurston's four years later in 1926 to be well beaten by Newman again. He also lost to Newman in the 1927 final but was no longer getting thrashed; now he lost to the old champion by the respectable margin of 16,000 points to 14,763. More practising, and his reward came in 1928 when winning his first world professional championship, beating Newman by 16,000 to 14,874. He mastered Newman in the next two years and thrashed the New Zealander Clark McConachy in 1932. He would have continued ruling the billiards world but for the arrival from Australia of Walter Lindrum, the greatest of them all. Joe lost in close battles in 1933 and 1934. Davis and Lindrum had both mastered the close-cannon, the most prolific scoring stroke invented. Joe jokingly told me he had worn out a new pair of trousers sitting through three whole sessions totalling three and three-quarter hours while Lindrum made a break of more than 4,000.

When Lindrum left Britain for the last time, the world billiards championship virtually died. It was at the twenty-two ball game that Joe was to become the champion of champions. He preferred the more bellicose snooker and was quick to realise that it would attract bigger audiences than billiards, and he managed to persuade the Billiards Association to sanction the first world snooker championships in 1927. Prior to this, Joe had only been able to popularise the potting game by persuading billiards professionals to play exhibitions as a fill-in when the billiards matches were over.

For those first world championships, there were only four entries including Davis, who also acted as organizer. Joe at 26 claimed to be the first world champion and received a cash prize of £6.10s. The old billiards professionals could not accept that snooker was here to stay. Tom Reece, who once scored a half a million break with his pendulum cannons, which were later barred, regarded snooker as a monster and suggested Joe should wear clogs and corduroys for the new-fangled game. This sarcasm did not deter Davis. He was a star years ahead of his time who promoted the game even without shrewd promoters and agents, and although he benefited himself, all the professionals of his day owed a tremendous amount to his 'showbiz' approach. Joe knew he could perform better than any other player in the world and that snooker would bring bigger crowds through the box office than the slower game of billiards; without the aid of television, snooker became well established with the public almost entirely because of Joe. Not a tall man and just a little tubby, potting suited his short, crisp cue action and aggressive attitude. He possessed natural talent for screw and stun shots which enabled him over the years to build up many record breaks. Shortly before the last war he set up a new world record break of 137; as always with Joe, he had to beat records, whether created by a rival or by himself, and a few weeks later he broke his own record with 138. Joe frequently cleared the tables and on several occasions I have felt sorry for an opponent who was not even given the chance to get to the table before the frame was won in lightning time. His name became magic and I have met many politicians, wealthy businessmen and personalities who would pop into Leicester Square Hall if they knew Joe Davis was in action. Because of his magnetism, snooker was to replace billiards in most clubs, pubs and billiards halls.

Joe held his world snooker title from 1927 till 1946 (it was not competed for between 1941 and 1945)*. Then he announced his retirement after twenty years as champion, and up to that time undefeated in a competitive game. He could probably have remained world champion for another decade. What is remarkable is that with all his tournament wins he played from scratch while most opponents received a generous handicap.

**Snooker world championship holders*

1927-46	Joe Davis
1947	Walter Donaldson
1948	Fred Davis
1949	Fred Davis
1950	Walter Donaldson
1951	Fred Davis
1952	Fred Davis
1952	Horace Lindrum (unrecognised by the Players Association)
1953	Fred Davis
1954	Fred Davis
1955	Fred Davis
1956	Fred Davis
1957	John Pulman
1958-63	Not competed for: title retained by John Pulman
1964-68	Title retained by John Pulman against all comers
1969	John Spencer
1970 (1)	Ray Reardon
1970 (2)	John Spencer
1971	Not competed for
1972	Alex Higgins
1973	Ray Reardon
1974	Ray Reardon
1975	Ray Reardon
1976	Ray Reardon
1977	John Spencer
1978	Ray Reardon
1979	Terry Griffiths
1980	Cliff Thorburn
1981	Steve Davis
1982	Alex Higgins
1983	Steve Davis

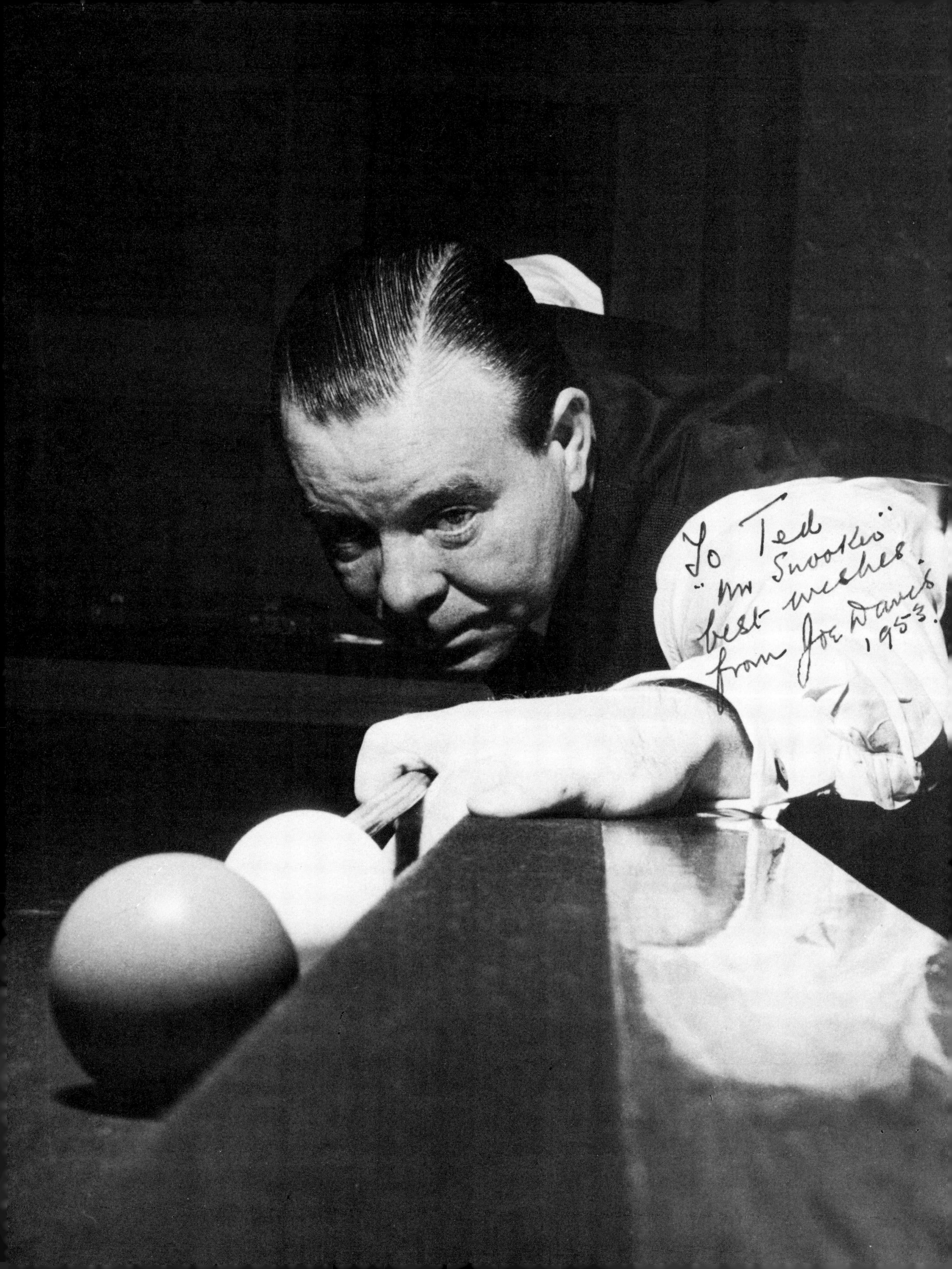
To Ted
"Mr Snooker"
best wishes.
from Joe Davis
1953!

One example of his determination and pride was when his world record break of 141 was beaten by George Chenier in Britain with 144. Joe allowed it to be only a temporary success for the French-Canadian. Three weeks later Davis made a break of 146 at the Houldsworth Hall, Manchester. And guess his opponent? Yes, George Chenier. That challenge brought the best out of Joe and he achieved it despite being snookered on the brown and having to pot that ball off a cushion. I still hear old-timers talking about the incident. Just to prove it was not a fluke, Davis shortly repeated a 146 break; but he had to wait nearly eleven more years to register 147. As he got older, this target became an obsession with him. And as the final curtain was about to fall at the Leicester Square Hall in 1955, playing against the veteran Willie Smith, Joe eyed the twenty-two balls and decided to have a go by ignoring any red that would not, after potting, put him on the black.

The maestro was more than likely to clear the table but on this occasion every priority was aimed at breaking his own record and becoming the first man to make a 147 break under championship conditions. All went well for him until he had scored 104 when he left himself on the wrong side of the fourteenth red. The cue ball was tucked between the red and a top pocket. Both balls were on the side cushion with only an inch or so between them. His only hope was to drive the red almost the length of the side cushion more than ten feet into the 'blind' baulk pocket against the nap of the cloth. I reckon any bookmaker would have offered 100 to 1 against Davis succeeding. Joe literally sweated and fretted over the position he had left himself in, longer than for any shot played in his life. You could have heard a pin drop and I felt my own fingers shaking with the tension. But he played it and as the red dropped into the pocket, a relieved Joe, playing faster than even Hurricane Higgins, scrambled the remaining balls into the pockets as though he believed that the slightest hesitation could cause him to fluff a shot. As the last ball went down, even the seventy-year-old dour Northerner Willie Smith flung his arms round Joe's neck, and the crowd stamped their feet for the first and last time at Leicester Square.

This was the only time in all the years I had known Joe that he revealed nerves. When the cheering had died and we began to move from the table to my office, he gasped: 'Ted! For God's sake pour me a large brandy'. After sinking it even faster than the last black in his 147 break, he 'phoned his wife June, who knew how much that maximum break meant to him, and told her the good news. Understandably enough, she burst into tears.

Apart from Joe and June, I was the only other person who knew just how much that 147 effort had taken out of him and when the tension had completely gone some hours later over a celebration dinner, he summed it up:

> 'I played some terrible positional shots as the chance of achieving this record became more possible. I cannot ever remember having been in such a state of

(Facing) Joe Davis, the King of Pot. The picture emphasises Joe's left-eye sighting; his right was weak from childhood.

> nervousness and near panic in all my career. After putting two long pots into the baulk pockets at 32 and 80 and each time screwing back for the black, I lost position hopelessly at 104. With thirteen reds and blacks potted, I found the cue-ball between a red and the top pocket on the side cushion with only an inch or so between them. I heard the spectators sigh with dismay. The break looked all over. I had only one chance. It meant I had to drive the red straight down the side cushion more than ten feet into the blind baulk pocket. My heart was beating fast and I found it almost unbearable as I hesitated, taking more time than for any other shot in my life. Yet as the red passed the centre pocket, I knew it was in. I was now excited and sank the last few balls as fast as I could. But how I suffered before it was all over!'

Joe always kept meticulous records of his feats. Early in 1953, when he was fifty-two, he mentioned to me over a glass of sherry that he had made 498 centuries and would be making his 500th in a tournament in Manchester the following week. Now, as general manager of Leicester Square Hall, I always had an eye to business and knowing that no player had scored 500 centuries before, I suggested to Joe that it would attract more publicity if he achieved this magic figure in London in a couple of weeks' time. The old wizard grinned and replied: 'I think you may be right, Ted. I'll certainly make one century in Manchester and the 500th at Leicester Square'.

So I 'phoned Bill (later Sir William) Carr, *News of the World* chairman, whom Joe, as a snooker contributor to that paper, knew well. Joe and I had earlier persuaded Mr Carr to get his paper to sponsor the £1,500 handicap tournament. I suggested he might care to attend a dinner for a few sporting friends to honour Joe on a fine achievement. He told me to come to his office but looking me coldly in the eyes he inquired: 'What do you expect me to do about it?' I was taken by surprise by his lack of enthusiasm but, knowing his great ego, I diplomatically said off the cuff: 'I thought you might be kind enough to take the chair on this occasion, sir'. He changed his attitude and said that as I knew a lot of people, I should find nine willing to buy ten tickets at £10 each. He then tossed me a cheque for £100 and said: 'Here's mine for a start'.

As always, the old maestro scored the centuries to order—the 499th late in a match at Manchester and the one we wanted at Leicester Square. Instead of the intimate dinner party I had originally planned to honour Joe's Five Hundredth Century, we ended up with 176 guests and a full cabaret at the Dorchester Hotel in London. And instead of the silver ash-tray I had in mind, Joe was presented with a gold cigarette box. Inside was a diamond and ruby studded watch for Joe's wife. Table cloths were set up in red, yellow, green, brown, blue, pink and black, and 176 ash-trays looking like snooker balls and inscribed 'stolen from the Joe Davis dinner' were there for the taking!

Davis was dedicated to his game and seldom took a drink before an important championship but, like myself, enjoyed a drink when off duty and in his social moods was great fun. I remember one evening after he had finished at Leicester Square, Joe suggested we should retire to the nearby Queen's cocktail bar. We were both relaxed and one drink followed another, and inevitably we decided to go on the town and finished in a nightclub drinking champagne until four o'clock next morning. I awoke a few hours later feeling fragile but remembering I had promised to call at Joe's house in Kensington as June was to help out with some letters in connection with the charity tournament. Joe could hardly keep his eyes open and June made some black coffee to liven him up before he went off to Leicester Square while we organised our letters. She was obviously a little concerned as Joe seldom had hangovers and asked me if I would ring the hall and see how things were. I 'phoned a member of the staff and discreetly inquired how it was going and whether Mr Davis was in good form: 'Terrific!' came the reply. 'He's just cleared the table with 131 in the first frame'. June was relieved. Knowing Joe, I wasn't worried but out of curiosity I 'phoned again to be told he had cleared the table in the second frame with 108. It had become such a joke that I 'phoned a third time and Joe had cleared the table for a third time with 128! What a professional! The hangover was self-inflicted so Joe had to prove to himself that he could turn it on under any conditions. He had a good sense of humour and a quick wit. One day he had scored 106 and missed what should have been a simple shot for him. A wealthy businessman who knew him said, not unkindly: 'Joe! Even I could have got that one'. As quick as a flash Davis counter-punched: 'Sure you could—but could you have scored the other 106?'

Away from the billiards table, Joe was a tremendous sportsman. He loved golf and racing. It was strange, though, that although a good golf player, his putting let him down. How he loved racing. When his playing days were over, he always dropped into the Allied Breweries' box at Ascot for a drink and information on a possible winner. One of my last memories of Joe is of him sitting in our box, watching a race on TV through binoculars. It was a reminder to me of the handicap this great player performed under. He had always had one bad eye and at times confessed he was almost blind in one eye. It was when his good eye began to trouble him that Joe, without ever losing the title, abdicated. And yet this champion of champions made 687 centuries, and eighty-seven breaks of more than 1,000 at billiards.

Joe's greatest asset, next to exceptional talent, was his ability to shine whenever he chose, as when scoring his maximum 147 in the last match at Leicester Square, taking the world record back from George Chenier, scoring a century on TV when sixty-one, or knocking up 141 against Jack Rea at Blackpool including 100 in 4½ minutes—his fastest century. Only one man ever beat him at snooker on level terms and that was his brother, who managed it three times when Joe was in the twilight of his career.

He was so upset when the Leicester Square Hall closed that he approached the Automobile Association and purchased the two swinging doors of the famous hall and had them installed at the billiards room of his home, saying: 'I feel two old friends have come to stay'.

Joe Davis's talent, charisma, energy and foresight were such that even when Leicester Square was no more, he was determined the game should not be allowed to collapse as it had done after the bombing of Thurston's, so he organised the first post-war world championships at the large Horticultural Hall at Westminster. More than 20,000 turned up during the fortnight, paying around £12,000.

In the final Joe, then forty-five, successfully defended his world title twenty years after he had first won it, beating Horace Lindrum by 78 frames to 67 in the final. The King made six century breaks and abdicated, but remained for many, many years 'Mister Snooker' as chairman of the Players Association and the game's most dominant personality. He could still beat the champions who followed him, but without him the world championships deteriorated rapidly and in a decade had become almost non-existent.

Joe's tremendous service to the game was rewarded with an O.B.E. I shall never forget when he collapsed from a heart attack at the Crucible Theatre, Sheffield, in April 1978, while watching Fred in a tense semi-final of the world championships. Two days later he survived heart surgery but was never the same man again. I visited him in hospital in the July a few days before he died. I knew it was to be the last time I would talk to a sporting king whose triumphs, disappointments and personal friendship I had shared for more than thirty years.

Horace—uncrowned king

WHEN Joe Davis retired in 1946 we all wondered what would happen next. Both Horace Lindrum and Fred Davis had lived in the shadow of Joe and we expected that one of them would be the first new champion for twenty years. Joe made no secret that he hoped, and expected, Fred to keep the title in the family; but as it happened a dark horse from Scotland named Walter Donaldson came up on the rails to beat them both, and it was not until 1952 that Horace Lindrum won the official world title. Even then his fellow professionals did not recognise his title because the dispute at the time between the Professional Billiards Players Association and the Billiards Association and Control Council, who organised the championships, meant that all the professionals except Lindrum and New Zealander Clark McConachy had boycotted them. However, this pair met and the Australian Lindrum beat McConachy 94-49, and his name is on the trophy.

However, it would be quite wrong to devalue Lindrum, for he was among the most attractive billiards and snooker players I have ever seen and had a twinkle in his eye, an ever-ready smile and a personality that stood out like a beacon. Only a phenomenon like Joe Davis prevented him winning an undisputed world title. His style was a combination of Hurricane Higgins and Steve Davis and nature gave him another advantage as a snooker player. He was double-jointed in all fingers. This allowed him the perfect bridge since when

Horace Lindrum, described by Ted Lowe as one of the 'most attractive players I have ever seen'. Horace's name appears on the trophy for 1952, when he beat Clark McConachy after other professionals refused to enter because of the dispute between them and the B.A. & C.C.

his fingers were spread flat on the table at full length he could raise his knuckles from the cloth with all four fingers gripping the green baize. I don't know of any other top player blessed with such a physical asset. It also allowed the Australian to be an expert with finger spins and he could play a brilliant exhibition without a cue, using his double-jointed fingers for running side, screw, follow-through or any shot for which another player would not only require a cue, but also a hell of a lot of chalk!

The name of Lindrum was as famous in Australia as that of Davis in Britain. Horace's great-great-grandfather won the Australian billiards title which remained in the family for many generations. His grandfather Fred was a super player, and then came his uncle Walter, the great billiards player. In fact, the title stayed with the Lindrums until Horace announced his retirement in 1957, relinquishing the Australian billiards and snooker titles. He came out of retirement in 1963 and won the Australian Open snooker title again.

Oddly enough, Horace was not born a Lindrum. His real name was Horace Norman William Morrell. He was born in Sydney on 15 January 1912, but after his parents divorced he changed his name by deed poll to Lindrum—his mother's maiden name. Behind his charming manner was a shrewd business head. He began playing billiards at twelve and had twenty tables to choose from, all owned by his grandfather who ran a billiards parlour in Sydney. Before he reached fourteen he claimed his first century. By twenty he had knocked up a four-figure billiards break of 1,431 and at twenty-one claimed his first snooker century of 139. Australia accepted this as a world record as it was made on a standard table but Horace, young and impetuous, did not go the right way about getting the B.A. & C.C. to recognise it and was very annoyed with them when they did not.

He was the original globe-trotter. As a schoolboy, he was a marbles champion (perhaps those double-joints helped him!) and he travelled thousands of miles through Australia; the Bush held no fears for him. Billiards broadened his travels. He was the first professional to visit New Guinea. Next came Britain, followed by journeys to Canada, New Zealand, South Africa, Rhodesia—as it then was—and India.

His happy personality was attractive to the ladies. But the girl who caught his eye was Joy White, one of the secretaries with the B.A. & C.C., and they were married at St Martin's-in-the-Fields, London, in 1949. After the bombing of Thurston's, we were all pretty hard up. We couldn't afford a car for transport and travelled mostly on the Underground. We spent our leisure hours playing in the Beaufort Club, off Lisle Street, near Leicester Square. It had an odd membership: taxi-drivers, stage stars and even a member of the royal family occasionally attended. It was owned by a large colourful character named Tommy

Horace Lindrum and Joy White marry in 1949.

Leng. Tommy, an original Grade A referee, loved snooker and befriended many players, including Horace. He was wealthy. He could produce the pound of butter, bunch of bananas, joint of meat or nylon stockings in the days when such goods were impossible to come by legitimately. One day 'T.B.,' as he liked to be known, was playing with Lindrum and I had challenged the winner when he announced that he was making a present of a Triumph Roadster to Horace to enable him to get to the many exhibitions he was playing, made difficult because Lindrum was without transport. Lindrum received his car and was delighted. Leng, however, was a man of many moods who frequently went on alcoholic benders for a week at a time. During these episodes he was difficult to handle and became aggressive. It was during a bad drinking bout that he turned up at his club one day when I was playing Horace. He turned on Lindrum, accused him of ingratitude and demanded the cash for the car he had given him eighteen months earlier. The Australian had been enjoying a successful tour and had sufficient cash to pay for the car. But they never spoke again.

Horace Lindrum is happy with the sports car given to him by Beaufort Club Boss Tommy Leng.

I mentioned earlier how I had patched up a breach between Horace and Joe Davis in 1970 before Horace and Joy returned to Australia. I was shocked to hear of his death in 1974. He was only sixty-two and had seemed such a relaxed player that I imagined he would see out the average man's span of three score and ten years. I still see Joy, who has now married again, on my annual visits to Australia. In a recent letter from Narrabeen Heights in New South Wales she wrote:

> I am always delighted to help keep the name of Horace Lindrum in the news. He was a good man who helped a great many people and never looked for credit or

> reward. Maybe it was unfortunate for him that his make-up was completely individualistic. Because of this, he suffered financial loss and, possibly, professional friendship.
>
> Horace sought to live his life in a fit and just manner. For this, one must admire his strength of character. It requires greater courage to follow a conscience when it is obviously more advantageous to follow the crowd. Integrity is a rare commodity.

I endorse Joy's remarks. He was a lovely man who played professionally for forty-two years. When he was fifty-eight in 1970 he claimed to be the first player to make 1000 snooker centuries in public performances. It would take too many pages of this book to do him justice but I have picked out a few highlights of his career. He was certainly the best snooker player I have had the pleasure of working with who wore a synthetic crown; for the Players Association still do not recognise him as a world champion.

Donaldson—the lone Scot

THE EXPERTS who tipped Fred Davis or Horace Lindrum to become the first new world champion for twenty years after Joe Davis's abdication were all wrong. The first man to wear the crown in 1947 was Walter Donaldson, a quiet, balding Scot who had recently been demobbed from the Army after serving six years in the Middle East. Donaldson was not unknown to me prior to my joining Leicester Square Hall, but I confess I had never thought of him as a possible successor to Joe Davis. Walter later enjoyed success at the Albany Club in Savile Row, which was run by an Irishman called Bill Little and was an exclusive haunt for rich businessmen, Hollywood stars, West End entertainers, politicians and sometimes royalty. The Albany Club had a luxurious snooker room, and we suggested to Bill Little that it would be a good idea to run a tournament. He put up £500 and the top pros were invited; bets were struck in hundreds and sometimes thousands of pounds. Donaldson quietly took the first prize, beating Alec Brown in the finals by 20 frames to 11.

Walter had been playing billiards since the age of six. Though born in the suburbs of Edinburgh, his father had bought a hall in Coatsbridge and because of young Walter's persistence in wanting to get hold of a cue and hit the balls, his father built a platform round the most worn table and let his son practise with a cut-down cue every day for hour after hour. Having lived for the game, he was good enough to play his first game as a professional when only sixteen and in his twenties opened his own hall at Rotherham. It was here he met his wife Ida—she was the pretty young girl who lived in the house opposite his digs. A few years later he realised the first of his ambitions, becoming billiards champion of Scotland.

By 1933 he had switched to snooker and entered his first world championship. Although delighted to beat an old billiards opponent in Willie Leigh, Walter then came up against Joe Davis and was given the mother and father of a hiding. But he wasn't disheartened and kept plugging away; in 1939 he qualified to play at Thurston's, a boyhood dream come true, where he beat an established veteran, Claude Falkiner, and put up a good fight in the next round before losing to the accomplished Sidney Smith.

The Scot was improving all the time, but nearly six years in the war set back his game. Despite being rusty he entered the 1946 championships at the Horticultural Hall two months after he was demobbed. He was drawn against Joe Davis in the first round proper and was trounced 21-10. This defeat made him more determined than ever to catch up on the years of missed pratice while in khaki and with the help of a great snooker fan, Albert Brooks, who set up a snooker table in the loft of his bungalow at Belvedere, Kent, Walter spent his days and evenings practising. In the 1947 world championships the unobtrusive Scot was unbeatable. In the first round proper he beat Stanley Newman 46-25 at Wellington, Shropshire. At Liverpool he defeated Horace Lindrum 39-32.

I was delighted because I now had an attractive final at Leicester Square between Donaldson and Fred Davis, but then came a personal headache. The builders who had promised that Thurston's would be reconstructed and re-furnished by the first week in September had been held up by a shortage of material, labour and permits. The final had to be postponed until 1 October. Donaldson was not the least bit upset. He used the delay to get in more practice in the loft at Belvedere whereas Fred, more easygoing, was never a slave to homework. When at last Leicester Square Hall was ready I was a happy man. Every session of that final was packed and I had to turn fans away, many of whom arrived for the evening sessions in dinner jackets.

The final was played over two weeks and 145 frames. It was a dour battle. Donaldson led 44-28 after the first week. He refused to be rattled and, sticking to cautious, uncompromising tactics, stayed ahead of Fred and took his first world title by 82 frames to 63.

But the tension of winning and the months of non-stop practising was to take its toll and Walter began to develop headaches which worried him, interfered with his concentration and caused his game to deteriorate. Eventually, he consulted a specialist in Harley Street who diagnosed conjunctivitis and ordered complete rest.

It was cruel luck for Donaldson, who had to take months away from the game. He returned in an attempt to retain his title in 1948 and did well to reach the final, but was beaten 84-61 by Fred Davis. Fred beat the Scot again 80-65 in the 1949 final. To the credit of Donaldson's fighting spirit, he beat Fred 51-46 to win his second world championship in 1950, but Davis met and beat Walter in finals for the next four years. The pair dominated the championship after Joe Davis's retirement, meeting in eight finals between 1947 and 1954 with Fred winning six and Walter two. Fred later went on to win two more titles, beating John Pulman in 1955 and 1956.

I got to know Donaldson well after my first meeting with him in 1945 and the more I associated with him the better I liked him. His character, like his snooker, was straightforward and plain, without side. He was a lethal potter with a cue action similar to Eddie

Walter Donaldson goes upstairs to practise on the snooker table in snooker fan Albert Brook's loft.

Charlton, usually striking the cue ball in the centre, rarely using side, and was deadly on long pots. Strictly a family man, he preferred to leave a match immediately and drive home in his modest Ford Prefect to his wife Ida and son Peter rather than have a few drinks with the boys. In 1960, with the game at its lowest ebb, Walter realised he would never again win the world title and retired. He had already taken an interest in farming and decided to send Peter to agricultural college. Walter was happier on his farm than playing snooker in London. He kept a few pigs, cows and hens and had a 'hand' and his son to help him. Ida was also involved and enjoyed the life. The Scot turned to bowls for relaxation, reached county championship standard and played in the Middleton Cup. It was during one of these games that Ida brought their first calf into the world!

Walter encouraged Ida to take up bowls and she, too, became proficient. They enjoyed many hours together on the green until on 24 May 1973 Ida travelled to Denham to play in a match against Surrey and her husband, who had remained on the farm, had a sudden heart attack and was rushed to hospital. Sadly, the police had to interrupt the bowls match to tell Ida that Walter had died in the ambulance. My memories of Walter are like his life-style—quiet but very genuine.

Fred—relaxed statesman

HAVE there ever been two sporting brothers with more consistent records than Joe and Fred Davis? If Big Brother, twelve years senior, overshadowed Fred by remaining undefeated world champion for twenty years, the kid brother didn't exactly let down the family name by collecting eight world championships and carrying on at top-class level until nearly seventy.

It was a tremendous endurance test for Fred to play for so many years in the shadow of his more extrovert brother and then to have the patience and ambition to come good himself after Joe retired from competitive play. Fred was still a force in his late sixties, surviving two heart attacks and competing against the likes of Steve Davis when more than forty years Steve's senior.

Far more happy-go-lucky than Joe, Fred would shrug his shoulders or beam an engaging grin at an opponent or spectators even when under pressure. He had to overcome a big disadvantage from an early age because of bad eyesight. He solved his problems earlier by switching to swivel-joint spectacles which helped him considerably, and many years later he was even happier playing with contact lenses. I am convinced that had Joe not been such a super champion, Fred would have excelled far earlier, because he did not really assert his authority and desire to win until after Joe retired. Although they were always pals, there is no doubt that Joe was the boss in earlier days and did not rate Fred highly nor encourage him. This may have given Fred an inferiority complex, for he was certainly introverted when a young player and was twenty-four before entering his first world snooker championship in 1937, when he was beaten in the first round. Being extremely shy, Fred did not even confide in his parents or brother that he was having trouble with seeing the balls at a distance and was extremely worried about his hazy vision. At last he decided to consult an optician who came up with the suggestion of swivel-joint glasses. His game improved so much that he reached the semi-finals of the world championship in 1938 and 1939. In each case he was beaten by Joe. He went one better in 1940, reaching the final, again losing to his brother but by only 37 frames to 35. That was the last championship until after the war and Fred, having joined the Army, was restricted to exhibition games. When the war ended he hoped to succeed his brother as world champion but was surprisingly beaten in the 1947 final by Walter Donaldson. Fred's first world title came the following year and, apart from 1950 when the Scot won again, Fred beat Donaldson in six finals.

Unfortunately, the world title meant little in the 1950s, and once Leicester Square Hall had closed there was little to be earned from the game. Fred and his wife Sheila invested in a 100-bedroom hotel at Llandudno in North Wales and though Sheila ran it and Fred played snooker occasionally, he found it was not worthwile financially to defend his title in 1957. A young John Pulman took the championship for the first time that year.

Fred's contribution to snooker has been remarkable. Taking into account five years of war plus a further ten years of the game's recession, he was still able to hold his own with rising stars as an old age pensioner. Not only has he brought pleasure to spectators with his ability but he has added an old-world charm with his delightful relaxed smile and sportsmanship. Don't be fooled, however; behind that smile lurks an aggressive and determined mind. However, it was nice to hear time and time again a voice from the back calling out: 'Good old Fred!' Fred Davis also achieved something no other player could boast, beating Joe on level terms three times in tournaments. He had a cheerful enthusiasm which seemed to grow with age and when in 1981 he was preparing for the big snooker tournaments and the defence of his world billiards championship at the age of sixty-seven, his enthusiasm was as great and the twinkle in his eyes as bright as when he won his first world title.

When we started Pot Black in 1969, Fred was one of the first pros to be invited and he took part every year until illness forced him out in 1974. He never won this tournament but set up the highest breaks in 1970 and 1971 and on the second occasion finished runner-up to John Spencer. I was delighted when, after taking a long rest on medical advice, he told me he would be available for Pot Black in 1975, if invited. He played and again put up the highest break; he was still competing as late as 1979.

Fred is a quiet but stubborn man. After that illness which I thought would put him out of the game competitively, he was back at sixty-two challenging for the world title at Manchester in the spring of 1974, including among his victims Bill Werbeniuk and Alex Higgins before going down to Ray Reardon in the semi-final. As a 'senior citizen', Fred appeared in the 1978 world championships with contact lenses, defeating Dennis Taylor and Patsy Fagan before losing to Perrie Mans in the semi-final.

After his illness I told Fred that life seemed a little unfair and that I had received perhaps a better break than I deserved. He has been one of the cleanest-living men I have known. He never smoked and avoided heavy drinking, settling for a glass of wine, always watching his weight, believing that all things should be done in moderation. On the other hand, for a quarter of a century I had knocked around the clubs and pubs and hotel bars because it had been an occupational hazard as manager of Leicester Square Hall and later as a salesman and director of Allied Breweries. I confess I had done the lot—smoked, drank and over-ate, and often with only a few hours' sleep as I arrived home just ahead of the milkman. Yet there was poor Fred having two heart attacks and me in comparative good health for my age. I declared: 'There ain't no justice, Fred!' But he only beamed back and said: 'It's all a matter of luck and to do with one's stock. You are basically tough and seem to survive whatever happens. Perhaps it's the metabolism or chemistry. If you have an imbalance, you'll have problems no matter how carefully you look after yourself'.

Born in the same pub as Joe, Fred also became hooked on billiards as a child and though less dedicated, he won the boys' championship at fifteen and later became junior snooker champion three times. Fred annoyed Joe and shocked a number of friends by his slight scorn of coaching and practice. He believes that great champions are born and not made. If you aren't endowed with a natural talent, all the coaching in the world won't turn you into a champion. While Joe agreed with this theory, he did not accept that a player with talent did not have to practise for hours every day, and accused Fred of a lack of dedication.

Fred with all his success once told me: 'I seldom practise because no two tables are alike anyway. And I couldn't always tell a youngster how to play one of my shots because it comes naturally to me'. I respect Fred's honest philosophy and agree that the most important thing is to be born with a natural talent, but I would have to go along with Joe and

Fred, unlike Joe, had a light-hearted approach to snooker. Even when winning many world titles, Fred did not overdo the practice. Joe would practise for hours before important matches.

Fred and Ted: two very old friends, Davis and Lowe, get together before a game of pool.

most champions who insist on hours of practice to help a young player reach the top. Steve Davis, for instance, was meticulously coached by his father after Steve had, as a kid, studied Joe's book *How to Play Snooker*. Steve practised morning, afternoon and night. And this dedication undoubtedly helped him win the world title.

Though snooker has been the people's game for more than half a century, Fred never lost his early love for billiards. He had been United Kingdom champion for twenty-eight years before losing the title in 1979 when sixty-six. And the following year he beat Rex Williams, holder of the world professional billiards championship, in a challenge match at Leeds. So at sixty-seven, when many men have retired to their rocking chairs, Fred joined Joe as the only two players to have won both the world billiards and snooker championships.

In 1977, Fred, like Joe, was rewarded for his services to his sport with the O.B.E., thus rounding off a career in which he has received every honour the game could offer. He moved from Hampshire to a small stud-farm in Worcestershire, mainly for the sake of his daughters, Lynn and Alison—Lynn in particular is keen on horse-breeding, and Fred has always taken a keen interest in horse-racing. Sheila, Fred's dynamic wife, tragically developed Parkinson's disease in later years, and the family has now returned to North Wales. I hope this relaxed statesman continues to derive pleasure from the pleasure he continues to give us.

Pulman Express

I SHALL always look back on John Pulman as a young man who did a tremendous salvage job for the game when it needed it most. He was an exciting player who introduced fun into snooker at a time when black clouds threatened its very existence as a spectator sport. A handsome young man from Devon, with a swashbuckling attitude, he won the world championship eight times, defending it against all comers, any place or any time, just as long as they could find somebody sufficiently interested in putting it on in those days before the tobacco companies decided it was in their interest to sponsor sport. So to John goes much credit in keeping an ailing sport alive in an era of crisis.

Yet we might not even have heard of John Pulman had his father not made a decision to change his job, uproot the family and move to a new district. Mr Pulman ran a small baker's and confectionery shop at Teignmouth on the Devon coast, but he was ambitious and the profits were not sufficient for him to do all the things he wanted for his wife and two young children. So he sold the shop and moved to Plymouth to open a snooker club with nine tables. This was in 1929 when John was only six. By the time he was nine, he had an idea what the game was all about, using a small cue especially made for him. Then his father moved to Exeter and opened another club. Pulman senior, who frequently made century breaks at billiards, was now determined to coach John. He was an efficient but strict teacher. Young Pulman was not now allowed to pot a ball. Instead, he spent months hitting the cue ball up and down the table mastering the arts of side and pace. It was all rather boring for the lad who wanted to show how well he could pot a ball, but John will tell you today that but for his father's insistence on his mastering the fundamentals, he would not have reached the top. John had natural talent and made his initial 100 at billiards when only twelve. He was fourteen when he appeared in his first big event, the Boys' Billiards Championships at Burroughes and Watts in London's Soho Square. It was, in fact, his first trip to the Big City and he'll never forget his journey from Exeter, travelling alone before being met by an uncle at Waterloo Station. He was so excited and then confused when the passengers had to make an unscheduled change at Basingstoke that he left his own special cue on the first train and arrived in London a sad and worried boy. But the people at Burroughes, seeing his distress, were kind and allowed him to choose a cue from a large selection.

Though knocked out by a Wisbech lad named Barrie Smith, Master Pulman was allowed to keep the cue and played with it for many years. (Incidentally, the Wisbech boy who beat him grew into a fine professional under the name of John Barrie.) Like most youngsters, John found snooker more exciting than billiards and had become a splendid boy player when war came in 1939. Snooker, inevitably, took a back seat and the Pulman club at Exeter closed. When old enough, near the end of the war, he worked in an aircraft factory. Later he had a short spell in the Army before taking a job in an Inland Revenue office. Obviously, lacking in practice, he was anxious to get back into the game and joined the Conservative Club. The opportunity to show the locals how useful he was came when Fred Davis visited Exeter and John gave an impressive display. Through Fred he met Joe who gave the young Devonian much encouragement. But his greatest benefactor was a mutual friend, Bill Lampard, a wealthy baker from Bristol. Bill was a real enthusiast of the sport and also a member of the B.A. & C.C. He not only agreed to sponsor Pulman but set up a billiards room at his home outside Bristol, which enabled John to catch up on much of the practice he had lost during the war years. As a result of much dedication Pulman became English amateur champion at twenty in 1946 and turned professional later that year.

John spent every spare moment practising and made a fine impression in his first real season as a pro. His early triumphs were marred only by the fact that his father had died when only fifty-four and, therefore, never knew that all his early pre-war dedication to John's career was to bear such fruit. In 1948 the *Empire News* sponsored a snooker tournament for £1,000. Some younger players were required to make up the number and Pulman got his chance. He grabbed it with both hands, collecting £400 of the total prize money, which was only £50 less than Joe Davis earned for winning the tournament. This came about because John picked up £150 for winning the qualifying rounds plus £250 in the competition proper. John was improving all the time and was the up-and-coming star of the 1950s, reaching the final of the world championships in 1955 and 1956 but losing each time to the steady Fred Davis. He looked a winner in 1956 when leading 31-29 at the start of the final day but experience told and Fred ended up champion, winning 38-35.

Standing 6ft 2ins tall, the young Pulman was a stylish player who pleased the fans, who loved to watch him crashing the balls into the pockets. Like myself at that time, Pulman enjoyed the bright lights of the Big City and the clubs and the showbiz folk we met in them. We had a great deal of laughs together and I can remember in the 1950s being introduced to a small drinking club in Panton Street, between Leicester Square and Piccadilly. It was the 'in' place and its members and guests included top actors and actresses of the day. The famous Crazy Gang was regularly appearing at the Victoria Palace and we had tremendous fun with Bud Flanagan, Chesney Allen, Jimmy Nervo, Teddy Knox and Charlie Naughton. Teddy introduced us to the gambling game of Spoof, but insisted we used match-sticks and not money. Spoof—it boils down to guessing how many coins or match-sticks each of you have in your clenched fist and the man who names the correct total collects—it is a contagious game and John and I spent hours at it; unlike Teddy, we prefered to use money and in the years that followed in all our trips round the country we always enjoyed a session at Spoof.

The Crazy Gang give Ted a helping hand by publicising Long Life beer . . . John Pulman and Ted were taught the game of spoof by Teddie Knox and Charlie Naughton.

John finally became world champion in 1957, when Fred did not compete, beating Jack Rea 39-34 in Jersey. But, sadly for him, he had arrived as the right man at the wrong time and saw little of the advantages he deserved as world champion. The game was now at its lowest and television, though not interested in snooker at this time, was a new 'toy' to the public. The cinema, theatre and many forms of entertainment including sport were badly

In relaxed mood, John Pulman and Ted try to sink a glass of champagne. They both enjoyed a spot of fun when the games were over.

hit as people stayed at home glued to the 'little box' which was so much cheaper than a night out. Snooker was, I think, the hardest hit of any entertainment.

The world championship became dormant and with no promoters or sponsors the event was not competed for between 1958 and 1963. Despite this set-back, John Pulman showed himself to be a splendid champion and competitor. He didn't sit back but made it known that he was prepared to defend his crown against any challenger, anywhere that such a game could be staged. In 1964 he beat Fred Davis and Rex Williams. The following year he defended successfully against Davis, Williams and Freddie van Rensburg of South Africa. In 1966 he beat Davis and in 1968 held off the challenge of Eddie Charlton. The championship was resumed as a knockout competition after this and though Pulman never won another world title, he showed his fighting qualities as late as 1977, losing by two frames to John Spencer in the semi-finals before Spencer went on to win the title, beating Cliff Thorburn.

John Pulman did not have the luck bestowed on some champions all their lives. Apart from reaching his peak at a time when the game was financially dead, his marriage broke up and he had a severe car accident that threatened to end his career. Once again he showed fighting spirit by coming back after bad injuries to compete in the big tournaments, but he never quite recaptured his old form. Some of the youngsters earning fortunes today don't realise how lucky they are. The game owes much to Pulman for what he did in the sport's darkest hours. In his heyday he had an impeccable personal style. He cut a dashing figure with his hair always perfectly groomed, and dressed magnificently in evening dress with waistcoat and diamond and onyx cuff-links. His game was also elegant and though he had a long way to bend to reach the table, his stance was perfect, which he owed to his father's rigorous coaching. He would have been a natural star for colour television, with millions of fans, and no doubt would have financially matched the young millionaires of today.

After retiring from top-class tournaments at the start of the 1980s, John joined ITV's commentary team. Nobody has a better insight into the game he served so well for over thirty years.

Spencer, the cool cue man

JOHN SPENCER is the only world snooker champion who first played on a billiards table at Sunday School. He attended Radcliffe Sunday School, near Manchester, and in the recreation room they had a small billiards table. John became fascinated with the game and knocked up his first century when he was only fifteen. But he had no great ambition to become a world beater. In fact, he only played for fun and years later, when good enough to win the world title three times, he still played more for pleasure than for the prize. When called up for National Service at eighteen, he had no intention of taking up the game professionally, and it was ten years later that he entered the English amateur championship for the first time and did well enough to reach the final before losing to Ray Reardon. He lost in the final again the next year, but won the amateur title in 1966. He still had no intention of turning professional until after a dispute with the controlling body he withdrew from all amateur tournaments. When invited by the professionals to join them he responded quickly, and proved his class by winning the world title, trouncing Gary Owen 46-27 in 1969.

John Spencer could have been a matinée idol when he first came on the snooker scene.

His happy-go-lucky approach delighted everybody and he replaced John Pulman as the new star.

In 1970 the world title was competed for twice in Australia, and Spencer was beaten by Reardon in the final in the spring but was back in business again in November, beating Warren Simpson to win the title again and in such splendid form that he produced three centuries in four frames. He had been playing such entertaining snooker that he was one of my first recommendations for the launching of Pot Black in 1969, and as I have already men-

Spencer, who won three world titles between 1969 and 1977, is a great practical joker and has fun on the table and over a sing-song.

tioned, he excelled at the 'sudden death' competition, finishing runner-up to Reardon the first year, winning the next two years, and becoming the first player to win the event three times when he beat Dennis Taylor in 1976.

As with the young Pulman, it was always fun to go around with John Spencer. He has a tremendous sense of humour and it took me some time to work out when he was serious or just having me on.

When John won the world title at his first attempt I was convinced that he would dominate the game for as long as Pulman had done, but in the 1970s snooker was beginning to boom and attract more competition. Ray Reardon arrived to win the title six times, and Spencer had to be content with three—but he did have the satisfaction of breaking Ray's monopoly of the championship in 1977 after the Welshman had won four titles in a row. He beat Reardon 13-6 along the way and went on to defeat Cliff Thorburn in the final; it was quite a feat at forty-one to regain the title he had last won six years earlier. I don't think many viewers of that championship realised what a great achievement it was for the easygoing Spencer to motivate himself to win another world title after years in the wilderness.

John Spencer had one of the most pleasing styles of any champion I have seen. Perhaps it was because he was so relaxed and didn't treat winning as a matter of life and death that he possibly did not get in sufficient practice to stay at the very top. John's first job was in a betting shop and he always enjoyed a gamble or a day at the races. He was the first of the new regime to realise that snooker itself was becoming a tremendous gamble and would develop into a pressurised rat-race. In the old days there were but a handful of professionals; Joe Davis was able to dominate them for more than two decades. When John Spencer turned pro in the late 1960s, he was one of eight operating on the circuit. In less than ten years the number had increased to more than thirty, and the figure is still going up as more and more youngsters chase the ever-increasing prize money.

Spencer enjoyed his years at the top. Like all world champions, he was invited to travel the world and he once told me he reckoned he had journeyed a million miles between the ages of twenty-three and forty-three. He described himself as a lucky guy, getting well paid for having lots of fun. As a result of his success he was able to open his own club at Bolton in 1978 at a cost of around £70,000 and has the perfect partner in his wife Margo to take care of things whilst he is away. John's early success as a businessman probably helped cut short his career as a world-beater. He loved travelling and taking part in money-earning projects and well-paid exhibition matches. All these ventures delighted his bank manager but were not ideal preparation for world championships and big tournaments because exhibitions are played in very relaxed circumstances without any tension.

However, although John was just about the most relaxed world champion I have ever seen, even he realised when going for his third world title in 1977 that he was no longer the flamboyant player who had won his first title at the first attempt in 1969, and had some frights on the way to the final. He confessed to me afterwards that he had never known such pressure and during the thirteen days at the Crucible Theatre he lost nearly one and a half stone! Yet he showed no strain four days later when beating John Pulman 7-5 in the Pontins professional tournament to pick up the £1,500 first prize to add to the £17,000 he had earned winning the world championship.

I was a great admirer of John Spencer, who, like Joe Davis, reached the top without the aid of wealthy parents or shrewd agents. Like Joe, he was a self-made champion and businessman. It was always a pleasure to deal with John, who at his peak was an attacking player and an artist when it came to building breaks. He was not only relaxed when playing but also when talking to the media afterwards. He would give interviews freely and did not expect a newspaperman to have first made a deal with an agent before using a few quotes.

John joined the BBC's commentary team along with Rex Williams, Clive Everton and Jack Karnehm early in 1982. A good talker and wonderful interpreter of the game, he remains a shrewd and controlled gambler and, no doubt, learned much from his early days in a bookmaker's office. I know punters seldom broadcast their losses, but I know of two occasions when John has won £18,000 and £11,000 respectively on two horses.

His great sense of humour and showmanship was surely best illustrated when he made that 147 break on television in 1978 which the television boys missed. When he came to the last black, he lunged at the cue-ball as though he had tripped and missed. As the audience gasped, John smiled and winked at us—he was engaging in a spot of horse-play, but it took a lot of nerve. He proceeded calmly to pot the black to make a maximum 147 break—the first to be made on television but, alas, the cameras were not focussed on him.

John Spencer was not only a good champion but remains a splendid sportsman . . . and a habitual leg-puller.

Ambassador Reardon

RAY REARDON was something special in the world of snooker when he arrived in the 1970s. The struggling 1950s and 1960s had been ruled by Fred Davis and John Pulman. Then John Spencer came to the top and seemed booked for a long stay after winning the world title in 1969. But snooker wasn't quite ready for the sudden challenge of the black-haired Welshman. Ray was one of the really eager players from South Wales. He was only fourteen when he first went down the pits like those great Welsh boxing champions Jimmy Wilde, Tommy Farr and others. Boxing took boxers out of the pits and snooker did the same for Reardon. His father and uncles, like most miners, were addicted to the game. Beer and snooker were among the few pleasures the old miners enjoyed and every spare minute was spent playing or watching a chum playing in the Tredegar Miners' Institute. Ray was a natural from the start and entered the junior championships of Wales and England when only twelve. He won the Welsh amateur title before he was eighteen in 1950 and kept it for six years. He had an added incentive to succeed because Tredegar boasted of another young star in Cliff Wilson and as school pals and also in the Welsh and English championships the pair had some tremendous tussles.

In the beginning it was Wilson who seemed destined for the very top, winning the British junior title in 1952 and 1953, but as time went by Reardon improved more rapidly and became one of the most outstanding post-war professionals. The miners have always been proud to boast that Tredegar has produced world professional and amateur champions in Reardon and Wilson.

Though he had dominated the Welsh championship from the age of seventeen until he was twenty-three, Ray did not win the English amateur until he was thirty-two, when he beat John Spencer in the 1964 final. Surprisingly, this was a one-off success. Reardon's family left the Welsh pits and his father took a job at Stoke-on-Trent. Fate could have wiped out the snooker career of Ray Reardon because he was seriously injured when the roof of the Florence Colliery collapsed and he was buried for some hours.

Understandably, after this experience Ray decided to look round for less perilous work and joined the Stoke Constabulary; predictably, he won the Police snooker championship. Having won the English amateur, he developed the wanderlust when an opportunity arose for him to play in South Africa and he resigned from the police. He turned professional in 1967 and his pleasing personality and likeness to Christopher Lee in the role of Dracula all added to his box office value. Snooker's fans reckoned he was the loveliest Count Dracula of them all! He was an automatic choice for the first Pot Black tournament and won the 1969 event, also making the highest break into the bargain.

The Welshman began to make the biggest impression of any newcomer in the 1970s. He took the world title in 1970 for the first time when thirty-seven, beating John Pulman 39-34. From 1973 to 1976 he held the crown. His sixth world championship came in 1978 after a year in the wilderness when nothing would go right for him. He was determined to fight back and his concentration and deadly potting against Perrie Mans was fantastic. I still remember his coolness in the thirty-sixth frame after the South African had pulled back three frames to cut Reardon's lead to 18-17. He must have suffered inwardly when losing his grip on what looked a sure win earlier, but never showed a flicker of emotion on his face. Instead, he showed the stuff of which great champions are made by scoring the only century of the final—exactly 100—by taking that last frame 107-12. It was the crisis game of the match and, having re-established a two-frame lead, he took complete charge and finished up champion again by 25-18. Yet perhaps the most satisfying of his six world triumphs was in retaining the title in Sydney in 1975, when he had the task of beating the local champion Eddie Charlton.

Reardon has not only boosted snooker with his tremendous talent but he added bonhomie to the game. Just as Horace Lindrum and Fred Davis were loved for their boyish grin when something went wrong, so Ray has a way of friendly communication with the

Ray is also versatile in his own kitchen: here he is cooking up a surprise for his wife Sue.

spectators without allowing any interference with his concentration. There is always the flicker of a friendly smile when he has made a shot that has annoyed him and he gives his autograph more graciously than some of the stars. Unlike Alex Higgins, Ray can conceal his inner anxieties.

Having celebrated his fiftieth birthday in 1982, Ray has grown in stature and style and is generous to his victims, never discouraging youngsters like Jimmy White, and acknowledging his defeats with dignity and the reflection that on the day the other man

When it comes to golf, Reardon can sink a few balls.

deserved to win. Ray has not won the world title since 1978 and may never win it again with so many ambitious and talented youngsters on the golden trail, but even in his fifties Reardon will be the man many a young star will fear because age has not deprived the Welshman of his enthusiasm and the will to win, as he showed in 1979 and 1980 when along with Terry Griffiths and Doug Mountjoy he helped Wales to win the State Express World Cup.

In addition to six world titles, Reardon has won every major title apart from the Coral

U.K. and Jamesons and, despite a lean spell after winning his last world crown in 1978, he proved he was still an outstanding player by taking three major titles in the 1982-83 season. The revival came when after struggling for some years he won the first Professional Players' tournament at Birmingham, taking the £5,000 prize by beating Jimmy White in the final. The prize money was moderate for these days, but it was the players' own tournament and proved to him that his determination to keep practising had paid off and that he

Ray Reardon, most consistent champion since Joe Davis. Ray won six world titles between 1969 and 1978—four of them in succession. At fifty, the Welshman could still beat many of the champions half his age.

hadn't gone over the hill despite his seniority to White of thirty years. He then showed himself to be the grand master when he beat White for the fourth time in the season in the final of the Yamaha International Masters at Derby. Ray, trailing 4-6 after the afternoon session, fought back to win six of the first seven evening frames in the final and so beat his young opponent by 9-6. That victory was worth £12,000 to him.

Though Ray is by no means a poor man (thanks to the efficiency of his wife Sue, who acts as his manager) successes were gained when prize money was considerably smaller and, with the explosion in prizes, Reardon is determined to stay around to share in some of the jackpots the youngsters are chasing. And Jimmy White well and truly knows that no player in the world dare give the canny Welshman the slightest chance of getting off the hook, no matter how far he is behind.

Snooker has been good to Ray and he equally has been good to snooker and has been a splendid ambassador. Rarely does he upset anybody, but one comment made with complete honesty lacked his usual diplomacy. After coming back to beat White in the Yamaha, he expressed the opinion that Jimmy, being one of the greatest potters in the game, should not change his style as apparently some of his advisers wanted him to do. This brought a protest from Geoff Lomas, who works for the Sportsworld agency which handles the affairs of White. 'Ray is out of order', declared Lomas. 'Let him stick to running his own affairs'. Despite that little brush, I still regard Ray Reardon as snooker's finest ambassador since Joe Davis. And Joe was never afraid to speak his mind.

Ray and Sue, who have two children, run a thriving and successful business with irons in many fires. Ray's word in the snooker world is highly respected and he has toured the world, with no less than sixteen visits to Australia. He was a late starter in his chosen career but has achieved more in twenty years than most do in thirty.

The Hurricane blows hot and cold

WHAT can one say about Alex 'Hurricane' Higgins? Or what can't one say about the remarkable and unpredictable Irishman? He is the self-appointed People's Champion and sometimes self-destructive but, love him or hate him, he has done a tremendous amount to boost snooker and there has never been a better box office magnet. He is controversial, sometimes aggressive and not always popular with hotel managers if he decides to have a confrontation in the wee small hours. He is an extraordinary young man and if, like the rest of us, he has his share of faults, he can also be extremely pleasant and despite his mercurial temperament, he has undeniable talent.

Many stories have been told about the exploits of Higgins in Britain and Australia. Some of the stories are untellable, but it is taking the Hurricane a long time to blow himself out. He won his first world title in 1972 at his first attempt and ten years later huffed and puffed his way to a second world crown, beating Ray Reardon 18-15. In 1972 he collected £480 for his first world title. A decade later the prize was £25,000 and that win could be worth around £250,000 in business and perks.

Only the vodka-sipping, chain-smoking, nail-biting Higgins, often making no attempt to conceal pathos and dejection in defeat, could have turned victory into such an emotional soap opera for the 1,000 spectators at the Crucible Theatre and the 15 million viewers in their homes by insisting his wife Lynn brought their 16-month-old daughter Lauren in full view of the cameras to join in dad's triumph as tears dripped down his own cheeks. Even before the semi-final against Jimmy White he had insisted that Lynn should bring Lauren to Sheffield as the sight of his baby daughter inspired him, and he proudly carried her about to the delight of the press photographers as he told them: 'I'm going to win the title for Lauren'.

Higgins has been known to go to bed at 6am after an all-night party, but this time he went to bed early and rose at 6.30 to practise for three hours, which proves that at times he does not lack dedication. Jimmy White, known as the Whirlwind and said to have some of Higgins's wildness, was also well disciplined. He too went to bed early and did not take an alcoholic drink throughout the championship. He even surprised me by sipping milk from a glass during his match against Alex.

But it was Higgins who showed he had 'got a lotta bottle' because White, leading 15-13,

Alex Higgins's second world title was especially for baby daughter Lauren.

came within one frame of becoming the youngest player to reach a world championship final. Jimmy, in fact, needed to pot only one ball, having led by 60 points. It was then that the flamboyance and near-recklessness of the Irishman produced some of the finest snooker I've seen. He went for pots which few professionals would attempt and, sinking ball after ball, pulled back White's lead and, urged on by the approval of the crowd at his unbelievable fight back, made a 59 break—and Jimmy conceded.

Then the swashbuckling Irishman achieved what no other player has done in a world final. After leading Reardon 13-12 at the end of the afternoon session, then 15-12 and 17-15, when only a frame away from victory he registered a brilliant 135 clearance with poor Ray sitting as forlorn as a guest who had been invited to dinner only to find that the host has forgotten and gone out for the evening. No one previously had beaten Ray Reardon in a world championship final, with or without a century break.

Having showered praise on Higgins for his brilliance in the 1982 world championships, I don't wish to upset his many admirers, but must say his play at times resembles his lifestyle. He can equal the best with safety. He can pot balls that appear impossible and then turn in a sadly substandard performance—probably due to his nerves overtaking him. I have known him to be violently sick prior to a big match.

The nickname 'Hurricane' fits him perfectly and many of his wild exploits away from the table cannot always be dismissed as boyish fun. His drinking habits haven't always helped him and his very make-up is often contradictory. His moods are many. He can be charming and friendly and yet next day ignore you. But in all fairness to Higgins, he puts so much of himself into a tournament that the strain is clearly unbearable. Few people knew that when playing in a Benson and Hedges tournament in Dublin, he had been distressed by chest pains and was so worried during the tournament that he went to a hospital and was x-rayed. The doctor who examined him put the pains down to a form of nerves and the millions who have watched Alex on television are witness to the torture he inflicts on himself in an effort to win. The speed with which he pots when all is going well surely is also a form of nerves. It is to his credit that he overcame them sufficiently over a decade to win a second world title.

Higgins is his own man. He makes the rules and breaks them. Some of his tactics annoy the snooker world but few will deny his talent and that characters, even stormy characters, are needed to boost sport. Sometimes characters are their own worst enemies, but they do pull in the crowds. Alex Higgins is sometimes compared with George Best from the same city. There has not been a more talented soccer player in Britain than George Best since the 1960s. Both George and Alex collected more than their share of headlines—and not always on the sports pages.

It should never be forgotten that Alex Higgins had to survive in a tough district of Belfast. He had hoped to escape by becoming a jockey but put on too much weight and concentrated on snooker, which he had always enjoyed as a kid with the Belfast City YMCA; soon he was good enough to compete in the Belfast and District League. He had a flair for the game and sought to smash the balls into the pocket rather than concentrating on finesse. He played for hour after hour and never looked for coaching but taught himself by watching better players in action. A quick learner, he took the Northern Ireland amateur championship in 1970. He already had world championship ambitions and with persuasion and help from John Spencer became a professional and moved to England. Spencer's judgement was more than justified. Higgins won the world crown at twenty-three at his first attempt and was not the least embarrassed in 1972 to be interviewed on television in shirt and braces.

Higgins is a rebel and hasn't too much time for the Establishment. His antics have brought him fairly hefty fines from the World Professional Association and one feels that without his talent for snooker he could have become a dead-end kid. It is to his credit that he has made the effort to establish himself and become a wealthy young man. There must be thousands of kids in the slums of Belfast who watch the Hurricane on television and look up to him as their hero and are inspired to better themselves. Only a few will succeed.

Alex is a big contrast to Steve Davis, but make no mistake, he has a big following from those who admire the guts of a kid who overcame poverty to reach the top. The world loves an underdog and some women go for the little-boy-lost image of Higgins, loving to see him overcome all his anxieties during an important tournament. Alex has grown up in many ways in the ten years between his two world championship triumphs. Within a short time of his first triumph he decided to go on a barnstorming tour like Eddie Charlton has done in Australia. In an articulated lorry, the Hurricane took snooker and himself round the country, accompanied by John Spencer for exhibitions, complete with a billiards table and equipment and enough seating to accommodate 400 spectators. Higgins sells himself with the T-shirts, ties and badges of the People's Champion.

Alex Higgins is unique. He has learned to walk with kings and retain the common touch. He is happy when signing autographs for kids and hasn't forgotten he was once one of them. However, he is still tempestuous at times—especially after a drink when he can take exception to things. Yet he displays quite remarkable stamina and has been known to spend a night talking and drinking and still demolish the best opposition next evening.

His record in between his world title victories in 1972 and 1982 is impressive. He appeared in two losing finals against Ray Reardon (1976) and Cliff Thorburn (1980). Included in his successes were the Canadian Open (1975 and 1977) and the Benson and Hedges Masters (1978 and 1981) and the Coral U.K. (1983).

The U.K. Championships of 1983 produced a new, controlled Higgins. His epic final against Steve Davis, who took the first seven frames, will be talked about for many a day. Alex showed us all his artistry in capturing his first U.K. title, winning on the last frame after hours of tense 'to-ing' and 'fro-ing' of the lead.

Alex 'Hurricane' Higgins is the champion many love and some love to hate.

Can postman Terry knock twice?

TO BE classed a super champion at any sport, the individual must dominate all opposition and having won the world title, must defend it successfully several times to join the few outstanding champions whose records speak for themselves. Terry Griffiths was thirty before taking the plunge to become a full-time professional but was good enough to win the world title at his first attempt in 1979, with a convincing 24-16 win over Irishman Dennis Taylor. Terry, whose many jobs in South Wales included being a postman, has not knocked at the same door twice. Not yet at any rate. But though Terry is not likely to dominate the title as did Joe and Fred Davis, John Pulman or Ray Reardon, all in different circumstances, I shall remember him as a very good player who is also a nice guy.

Griffiths's introduction to snooker was a different one to most top professionals. His father did not run a pub or club. He was not coached at a very early age. Though only young when first playing in a hall at Llanelli, he participated just for the pleasure and had no early dream of one day becoming a world-beater. Yet by sixteen he was sufficiently proficient to play in the Llanelli Senior League. He had not changed his mind in his late teens and did not contemplate making a living out of it. Even after winning the Welsh and English amateur championships, he continued to hesitate when friends suggested he was good enough to turn professional for fear he might no longer enjoy playing, and was sufficiently humble to believe he would never be good enough to become a world champion.

Terry modelled his early game on Ray Reardon, fifteen years his senior, and the hero of every Welshman when he was the game's giant in the 1970s. Both have similar temperaments and such coolness under pressure is a tremendous asset. One of the biggest kicks Griffiths got was from winning the English amateur championship. Reardon had achieved the same years earlier and there's nothing a Welshman likes better than to capture an English crown!

Terry was twenty-four before he made his first 100 break. A year later he reached the final of the 1972 Welsh championships, losing to Geoff Thomas. He wasn't worried about losing but was, of course, pleased to avenge the defeat, beating Thomas to become Welsh champion three years later. The most important thing to Terry about this victory was that it enabled him to play for Wales and satisfy his urge for world travel, and in 1976 he represented his country in the world amateur championship in South Africa. Though beaten in the quarter-final he was delighted that another Welshman, Doug Mountjoy, became champion.

Mountjoy announced on the flight back to Britain that he was turning pro, but Griffiths's only ambition then was to succeed Doug as world amateur champion. He was honest enough to admit that if he changed his mind it would be because of the cash, but doubted if he had the dedication of Reardon, admitting he was basically lazy. To spend hours practising would become a chore and hard work for him. A devoted family man, he would not enjoy being away from home for weeks on end despite his ambition to travel the world.

So he still resisted invitations to join the pro circuit. He had worked in a colliery, been a blacksmith's mate, bus driver and postman, and tried selling insurance. Snooker was still for fun and he appreciated that his wife Annette, employed making radiators for British Leyland, was happy to be a wage-earner to help him travel for tournaments. Always modest, he was almost convinced that he belonged in the amateur world when he received 25 points from Reardon in the Pontin's Open tournament in 1975 and was dismissed 4-1. Ray went on to win the event, slamming John Virgo, who also received 25 points, in the final.

In his easy-going way, Terry shrugged off the defeat, accepting that Reardon was the champion of champions, and went back to Llanelli and relaxed with Annette and their children Darren and Wayne. He adopted the same attitude when winning the All-England final, crushing Sid Hood of Grimsby 13-3 in the final in 1977. Some said that Terry on the night was not just about the best amateur in the world, but the best player anywhere. He had won the sixth frame by the massive margin of 117-0 and seemed on the way to picking up the £1,000 prize Barry Hearn was offering to any player beating John Spencer's 102 break in the 1968 final; but Terry failed at 89 in the fifteenth frame. He expressed no disappointment but said his target was still the world amateur championship. He won the English amateur again, trouncing Bradford's Joe Johnson 13-5 in 1978, but was surprisingly beaten by Stan Newbury in the quarter-finals of the Welsh championships the same year. This cost him a trip to Malta to bid for the world amateur title for a second time and, rather than wait till 1980 for another crack at the world crown, after talking it over with Annette, it was decided he would turn professional. After all, Doug Mountjoy was doing well, having won the Coral U.K. and Pot Black in 1978.

It was amazing how Griffiths was able to switch from an uncommitted amateur into a dedicated pro. He made a disappointing debut, losing 9-8 to Rex Williams in the U.K. Championship after leading 8-2, but then the quiet Welshman settled down and shook the experts when, as an outsider, he won the 1979 world title and the £10,000 prize. His final win over Dennis Taylor must have been worth £50,000 to him that year.

It had not been a great final because Dennis and Terry, comparative unknowns, were playing it cautiously. Both were mentally and physically drained from the strain of two weeks spent eliminating the top professionals. In fact, Sheffield's Crucible Theatre was in danger of becoming, like the old Liverpool Stadium in the boxing world, the Graveyard of Champions, until Steve Davis won the title again in 1983. Reardon, having taken six world titles in nine years, was eliminated in the quarter-finals by Dennis Taylor in 1979. Griffiths went out in the second round against Davis in 1980 when Cliff Thorburn won the title. Thorburn was knocked out by Steve in the semi-finals in 1981 and Davis won the crown. In 1982 Steve was massacred 10-1 in the first round by Tony Knowles in the biggest shock for many years.

But nothing can take from Terry's glory in 1979. A rank outsider, he was almost a stranger to television fans. He had abandoned his relaxed 'it's only a game' attitude and played every shot as though his life depended on success. After all, he had been a working man all his life and now at thirty he needed to turn his beloved sport into a strict business not only for himself, but for his wife and family.

He became a new TV personality after only a few appearances. His gentle charm and good manners made him an instant friend of millions and as the championships progressed he was proving that there was not such a tremendous gap between a very good amateur and a good professional. He was at his best in the quarter-finals against Alex Higgins. The Irishman finished the first session leading 6-2 and the onlookers sat back for the inevitable elimination of the new boy. But for all his quietness, Griffiths revealed tremendous tenacity and took the first three frames in the next session, and though the Hurricane kept ahead at 8-5, the warning came when the Welshman made a 121 break and led 9-8. Higgins now had to battle for his life and the atmosphere was tense as it went to 12-12 after Higgins made a 60 break. The Hurricane missed a red in the final frame and paid dearly for it as Terry cleared the table with 107 and won 13-12. Another titanic struggle followed against Eddie Charlton in the semi-final with the Australian edging in front for the first time at 16-15. Again by sheer guts the Welshman struck back to win 17-16 and a passport to the final. As he turned from the table after the last ball went down, he endeared himself to millions by letting all the tension evaporate as, grinning from ear to ear, he declared in his marvellous Welsh accent: 'I'm in the final now, you know!' It brought the house down. The last match was as dour a final as I've seen, with both men desperate not to make any mistakes; the score stood at 15-15, but then Griffiths revealed star quality, winning nine of the next ten frames.

The nice thing about Terry Griffiths is that success has not changed him, and he was philosophical when eliminated by Steve Davis in the world and U.K. championships the following year, and in the world championships quarter-finals in 1981. He never offered any excuses for defeat, treating triumph and disaster as equal impostors. A strict teetotaller, Terry doesn't even keep a record of his century breaks. He knows 142 is his highest and guesses he has made about 300 centuries, but he couldn't be sure.

Griffiths didn't sweep all before him after his initial success, though he played a big part in the Welsh victory in the first State Express World Cup and took the Benson and Hedges Masters in 1980 as well as helping Wales retain the Cup. His best win was to take the U.K. title in 1982 after a long struggle against Alex Higgins. Trailing 13-15, Terry showed his old fighting spirit to win the last three frames.

Does the happy amateur of Llanelli regret turning professional at thirty? Is his new wealth worth all the pressure, the travelling and the continual challenge of youngsters? Griffiths has no doubts. 'All my life as a working man I switched jobs to earn enough money for my family. That is what I call real pressure. By comparison playing in top snooker is money for old rope'.

Terry Griffiths, collier, blacksmith's mate, bus driver and postman, at least appreciates the golden age of snooker. Most fans hope the postman will knock twice.

Teetotaller Terry Griffiths relaxes with his cup of tea—he won't drink coffee.

Thorburn—hustler to champ

CANADA's first success in the State Express World Cup in 1982 was inspired by the determination of Cliff Thorburn to break through to the top, which he did when beating Alex Higgins to become world champion in 1980. Fellow countrymen like young Kirk Stevens and Jim Wych agree that Cliff had been their hero for some years and his triumphs in Britain led them to follow him across the Atlantic. Big Bill Werbeniuk had already moved to Britain.

Some greybeards still insist that George Chenier from Montreal was Canada's greatest snooker player, and while I go along with them that George was a super performer, I would have to give Cliff Thorburn the No. 1 spot. It is, of course, impossible to come to any definite conclusion with such comparisons. The conditions of the 1940s and 1950s had changed beyond all belief by the 1970s and 1980s. Chenier ruled supreme in his own country as North American champion and compiled seven maximum breaks in his career, but wasn't up against the competition as is Cliff today—though much credit must be given to the French-Canadian for maintaining such a high standard without the incentive of real competition. In his only bid to win the world championship he came to Britain in 1950 but was beaten 43-28 by Fred Davis in the semi-final at Oldham. But he showed himself to be a splendid player, beating Joe Davis and Sidney Smith in exhibition games, making a century break against Sidney (121) and setting up a new world record of 144 against Joe. He was still accepted as Canada's champion when he died in 1970.

Canada always had good players like Conrad Stanbury, Jimmy Reed, Leo Levitt, Edward Agha, Vic Kireluk, Bernie Mikkelson, Paul Thornley and many more, but made its greatest strides with the progress of Thorburn, Stevens and Werbeniuk. England were really shaken when this terrible trio beat Steve Davis, Tony Knowles and Jimmy White at Reading in 1982. This was the first time an overseas team walked away with the World Cup.

Young Canadians refer to Cliff Thorburn as the 'Teacher' but he remains the same unassuming guy who, having begun as a 'hustler' in Canada, came here to prove he was in the world's top league. He once told me how, as a lad in Victoria, British Columbia, he was so broke that he frequently had to walk to work. One day he was given a lift by Cliff Kepner, a local sports star and Cliff's hero. Thorburn told Kepner of his problems and of his ambition to become a snooker champion. The star was impressed and loaned the kid twenty dollars which he obviously wasn't expecting to get back. In fact, they did not meet again for another sixteen years until Thorburn, then world champion, was playing at Hinckley, near Leicester, and Kepner, who had married an English girl and settled here, came and shook his hand. Now it was Cliff Thorburn who was the star.

Cliff began playing in a local pool saloon in Victoria and claimed his first century at nineteen and a 145 break at twenty. While it is easier to hit century breaks in Canada, Thorburn was good, as he proved on more testing British tables. He learned the hard way, taking any job, no matter how menial, to give himself the opportunity to earn a few dollars with which to gamble on himself at pool. He even worked as a dishwasher on a boat sailing between Victoria and Seattle. He also 'hit the roads' to Toronto and would play hour after hour in marathon matches. Although in a smaller way than Minnesota Fats, the famous pool hustler, Cliff some days could pick up 1,000 dollars—and still be broke the next day. It was living dangerously, but he found it stimulating—especially as snooker was the only way he knew of earning big cash. This tough apprenticeship stood him in good stead for the pressure when he beat Higgins in the 1980 world championships final to collect £15,000.

After winning the Canadian and North American titles, Cliff studied the styles of British stars like Fred Davis, John Spencer and Rex Williams when they toured Canada and it was Spencer who encouraged him to come to Britain in 1973 to bid for the world cham-

Cliff Thorburn proudly holds the trophy he won in 1980.

pionship. By 1977 he had improved sufficiently to reach the final, losing to Spencer. Three years later he was champion and the following year Canada took over Pot Black with Thorburn the winner, Jim Wych runner-up and Kirk Stevens bagging the highest break.

Despite his hungry days when desperate for dollars, Cliff found the two weeks of the 1977 world championships had so drained him in his tremendous fight before losing 25-21 to the more experienced Spencer that he could not sleep for the next six weeks. 1977 was the first year of the championships at the Crucible Theatre and Cliff had seen nothing like it before. He returned home and became a star in his own right, beating some of the best British players visiting there.

His ambition was fulfilled in 1980 in that tense final against Higgins, watched by fourteen million fans, with both players looking mentally and physically exhausted and unaware that while they were involved in a cliff-hanger the BBC had switched cameras to the siege at the Iranian Embassy. The 'Hurricane' was under such strain that he complained to the referee that the Canadian was interfering with his concentration by rattling the ice in his glass—a protest that was not upheld and which made Cliff more determined to win. The match had begun with a flourish by Higgins who led 5-1. Cliff fought back after trailing 5-9 to lead 11-9 and then the dog-fight began as the Irishman pulled it back to 11-11 and later led 16-15. But this was to be the year of the Maple Leaf. Playing inspired snooker, Thorburn scored a break of 119 and made fifteen breaks of more than 50 to lead 17-16; and as Higgins's face revealed complete torture and frustration, Cliff made a 51 break in the last frame, leaving Alex to set up five snookers on the last red—which meant it was virtually over before he sank the pink and black to win the frame 96-9 and the match 18-16. I have never commentated on a more tense final.

Cliff will give much of the credit for his triumph to his wife Barbara, a former sprinter with Canada's national team who once broke the 100 metres record. He admits that when he was young he was footloose and fancy-free, but it all changed when he met Barbara who, as a former teacher, is a good organiser and did a good job steadying him up and helped him become a better player. For a while they settled in England at Walton in Surrey and such was the change in his fortunes that Kirk Stevens also decided to try his hand in Britain. Cliff has not yet been able to repeat his success of 1980 and after a thin spell decided to move back to Canada to satisfy his wife's homesickness after their first baby was born.

Like Steve Davis, Cliff found the pressure of world championship snooker growing fiercer every year. He had made history, becoming the first Canadian to win the world title, and though in 1983 he created more history as the first to score the maximum 147 break in a world championship, he will remember those championships as the most traumatic in his career.

Cliff returned to Canada not only because his wife wanted to but also because he wanted to concentrate on regaining the tremendous form he had when he beat Higgins in the final. It seemed as though he had worked the magic at thirty-five, for in the first session of his 25-frame second round match against Terry Griffiths, the Canadian scored a maximum 147, worth £10,000 to him. He had claimed more than twenty perfect breaks, but they had all been accomplished in Canada where it is accepted that the pockets are larger and the balls lighter, and Cliff had never made 147 in Britain. What is remarkable is that the break began with a fluke!

The break—15 reds, 15 blacks and all the colours—happened in the fourth frame when Thorburn was leading 2-1. Griffiths had failed to contact a red and was penalised four points. Cliff aimed at a red but missed the pocket. The ball cannoned on to another red and went into a pocket. One felt that had Terry sunk the red earlier, he too might have made a maximum break because the colours were rather well placed, though Thorburn had one anxious moment after the fourteenth black when the cue ball seemed destined to finish behind the pink, snookering him on the last red, but it rolled on just enough for Cliff to wipe his perspiring hands and sink the last red into one of the centre pockets, positioning himself for his fifteenth black.

Thorburn celebrates after his maximum break of 147 in the 1983 championships.

The 147 had taken the Canadian 15 minutes and 20 seconds and, apart from the £10,000 prize, he received an additional £3,000 for the highest break of the event. The previous record in the world championships had been the 145 by Doug Mountjoy in 1981. Cliff's performance thrilled television viewers and virtually stopped the show at Sheffield. His countryman Bill Werbeniuk, playing David Taylor on an adjacent table, had to interrupt his own match to see Cliff complete the maximum and was the first man to congratulate him as Thorburn went down on his knees in the fashion of John McEnroe when beating Bjorn Borg to win Wimbledon.

This was the happy part of Thorburn's tense championships, but sadder incidents were to put even greater stress on him. Before beating Tony Knowles in a cliff-hanger semi-final he was to learn that his wife in Canada had lost their second child which she was carrying, which had been due to be born in the autumn. And he was involved in the three longest matches of the tournament, one of them not finishing until four o'clock in the morning. The Canadian began to show the first signs of strain during his match against Tony Knowles. Once he conceded the fifteenth frame and stormed off though in theory he could still have won. He admitted later that he could no longer bottle up his emotion after a friend told him about his wife's miscarriage. He was still edgy when resuming against Knowles next day. To his credit, he fought every inch of the way but Tony, suffering from nerves in his bid to reach his first world championships final, made some unbelievable misses which helped the Canadian to scrape through to face Steve Davis in the final.

Cliff came up for the final looking weary and baggy-eyed from lack of sleep. With Davis in brilliant form and ruthless mood, it was obvious there was to be only one winner as Steve built up a 12-5 overnight lead and continued to dominate the match to the extent that the proceedings were finished a full session early as he took six of the seven afternoon frames in storming form—to the embarrassment of Embassy officials, who prepared a four-man tournament to fill in time for the fans paying £10 for the final session. The triumphant Davis took part in the makeshift tournament while his party splashed the champagne about back at their Sheffield hotel.

Thorburn took his beating well but was, of course, depressed by his own sad domestic news and said at the end of the seventeen days' slog: 'Now I know what purgatory is like! I tried like hell but I knew deep down Steve was going to win.'

The Canadian had the consolation of taking almost as much cash out of the championships as Steve himself. And though crushed 18-6 in a dreary final, he came out of the event with a record break that can only ever be equalled, never surpassed.

While Bill Werbeniuk and Kirk Stevens, two Canadian bachelors, are around, Canada can challenge any nation. Big Bill is not only a splendid player but a great character and improved considerably after taking up a job as residential professional at Mike Watterson's Sheffield Centre in 1980. It may sound ironical to say of a guy whose weight varies between 16 and 18 stone that he lives in the shadow of Thorburn, but it is true. Without Cliff, Bill would have become Canada's top player and he has forced Thorburn to the limit many times. He is a happy performer and can sink a dozen pints of lager a day when in drinking form. He earned the biggest laugh on television when his trousers split during the world Team Classic. And his face wasn't even red!

Werbeniuk showed his power in 1982 when shattering England's defence of the World Cup title by beating both Steve Davis and Jimmy White. It was the first time Canada had won this tournament and they celebrated accordingly including showering me with champagne. It happened to be my birthday. He didn't turn professional till he was twenty-six and won his national title twice, and reached the quarter-final of the 1979 world championships to equal Rex Williams's highest break of 142 made in the 1965 championships.

Whatever the future of Thorburn and Werbeniuk, Canada has a young man ready to step in as the new golden boy. He is Kirk Stevens, as 'gorgeous' as any pop star, and as

Kirk Stevens, the flamboyant young Canadian star.

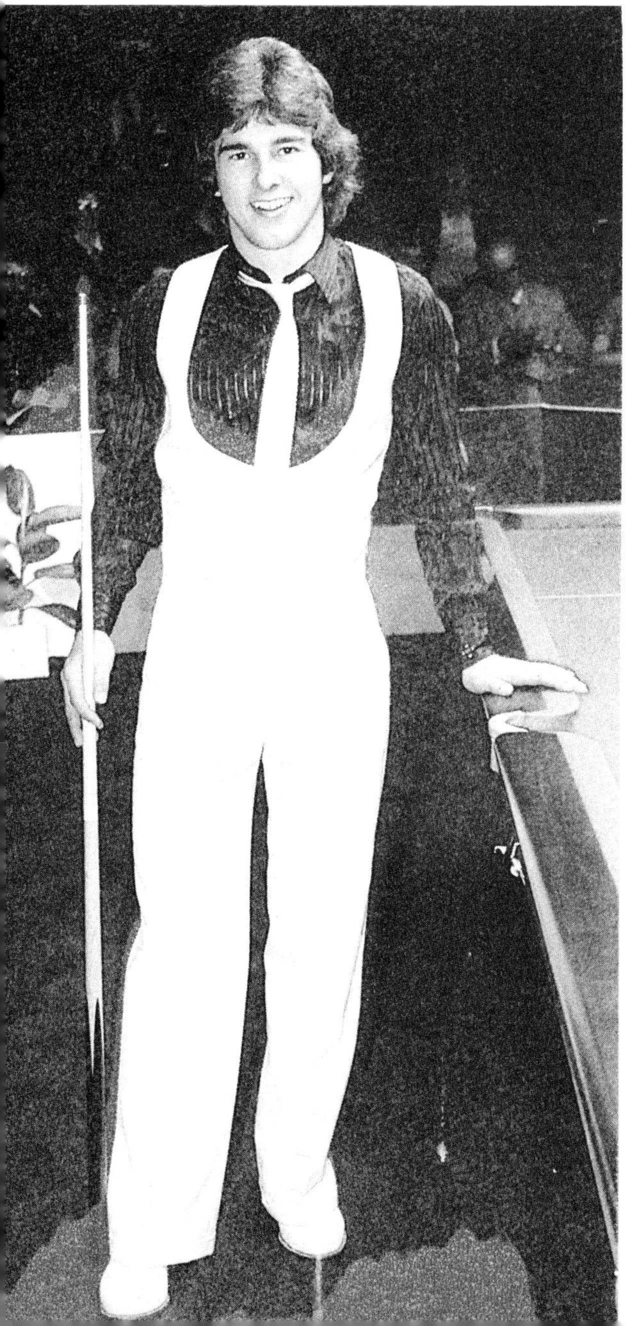

Big Bill Werbeniuk who thrives on pints of lager.

talented as any young snooker player I've seen. Brash but likeable, he claimed his first century break at thirteen, was a brilliant amateur and was barely twenty when beating Cliff Thorburn, the reigning Canadian champion, 7-5 to take the national title.

Kirk entered the 1979 world championships the same year that he won the Canadian title, and in the qualifying rounds beat Roy Amdor and whitewashed an out-of-form John Pulman. In the first round proper he was beaten 13-8 by Fred Davis but, staying for the World Cup, showed his potential by beating Ray Reardon and Gary Owen. It was his next World Cup appearance that put him on the map. After winning his qualifying rounds he beat Graham Miles in the first round and recorded a 136 break. He eliminated John Spencer and Eddie Charlton to become the youngest player to reach the semi-finals and also gave Alex Higgins a jolt, leading 5-2 before being eliminated 16-13. Kirk became an instant TV pin-up boy in his snazzy white suit. In the 1981 championships he eliminated Higgins, only to lose to Dennis Taylor. I was impressed and invited him for Pot Black 1981. He beat Steve Davis in his first game and though beaten by Thorburn and Reardon he took the highest break prize with 79.

As a teenager Kirk admits he was a ladies' man and the girls meant more to him than snooker, but by the time he was seventeen he was determined to become another Cliff Thorburn and the ladies had to take second place. He has tremendous talent and the good looks to make a million.

Canada has yet another young man on the championship trail in Jim Wych, an outstanding golfer and all-round athlete with a physical education degree. A left-hander, he took

Jim Wych.

the Canadian amateur title in 1979, joined the pros in 1980 and beat Kirk Stevens in the semi-finals of the Canadian Open before losing 9-6 to Thorburn in the final. He had a good run in the 1980 championships, beating John Bear and Rex Williams in the preliminary rounds and John Pulman and Dennis Taylor in the competition proper, only to lose to Thorburn again in the quarter-finals. In Pot Black 1981, Jim beat Eddie Charlton, Alex Higgins and Ray Reardon but was frustrated once more by Thorburn on that occasion. But who knows what may happen next with this talented player?

Steve Davis—clinical craftsman

THE sudden rise in 1981 of Steve Davis, a lad of twenty-three from Plumstead in South-East London, caused snooker fans immediately to compare the phlegmatic young redhead with Joe Davis. Yet apart from the pair sharing the same surname and the fact that Steve is one of the finest players since Joe ruled the snooker world, the circumstances in which each of them became world champion were very different. Steve not only won the world title for the first time but swept all before him in that year for an instant success story, a far cry from the long hard years of struggle that Joe, born in a small pub in North Derbyshire, had to undergo before settling down as a reasonably well-off middle-aged man. Life and the world have changed a great deal from the early part of the century when Joe was a boy determined to fight all the odds and become world champion; and whereas it took Joe a lifetime to be welcomed by his bank manager, and while the rest of the professionals of his day struggled to make a living, Steve and the young men who play with him are already affluent.

Steve Davis quit the Abbey Wood Comprehensive School with 'O' levels but decided not to allow studying for 'A' levels to interfere with his ambition to become a world snooker champion. Steve was first taught by his father around the age of five. Bill Davis, a London Transport worker, bought his young son a six-foot table when he reached ten and Steve's first association with a full-size table came when his dad took him to the Plumstead Common Working Men's Club. Davis senior, a useful player, realising how good young Steve was, dedicated himself to helping his son improve his game. Bill was then, as he is today, Steve's No. 1 fan and also his No. 1 critic. Steve says:

> 'Dad loves the game but he was a tough teacher. If I wasn't using the right technique, he would tick me off and, like most teenagers, I didn't like being told I was doing it all wrong and we had several ups and downs when playing together. Sometimes we got so tense with our differences that we wouldn't talk for hours, but I realised he was usually right and I would break the ice with 'Dad, now I see what you meant earlier. It was good advice'. He would grin and become even more enthusiastic with his tuition'.

While his dad coached him and encouraged him as a player, it was his mum Jean, an infant school teacher, who played an important role as a backroom girl. She did all the cooking and laundry, ironing his many shirts and pressing his suits to guarantee that his television image remained impeccable. It was family teamwork that led to the build-up of his victories, including the world titles in 1981 and 1983, that brought his gross earnings in three years to more than £1 million.

Steve's first big success came at 21 when, still an amateur, he won the Pontins Pro Am. In 1980 he hit the headlines, beating the world champion Terry Griffiths in the world championships before losing to Alex Higgins in the quarter-finals. Later that year he had a string of successes, beating Higgins and Griffiths again to win the Coral U.K. title at Preston. A

Steve at the table, 1981.

couple of days later he added the Wilson Classic,defeating the new world champion Cliff Thorburn, and went on to take the Yamaha International Masters and the John Courage English title. He was only twenty-three but had picked up £45,000 in prize money, and his earnings for the year were double this sum.

There was no stopping him. In 1981 he became world champion, having beaten Jimmy White, Alex Higgins, Terry Griffiths and Doug Mountjoy.

After Steve won the world championship, Bill Davis said:

> "We were, of course, delighted with Steve's achievement but when he comes home, my wife and I don't treat him like a world champion. He's our son. I'm still his dad. He may be a man and a champion to millions but at home he's still our boy and if he sits in my chair, I'll tell him so and he gets out of it quickly!"

Davis senior adds with affection that Steve isn't the most tidy person about the house:

> "Sometimes when he's at home it's as if a tornado had struck. I'm rather tidy myself, but I've learned to live with it. The great thing about Steve is that he has remained level-headed. He seems to enjoy playing the game even more than the money he earns from it. The first thing he did after becoming champion was to buy a house for us—nothing pretentious, just a nice little terraced house next door to my sister. We had lived in a flat since we were married and my wife longed to have a little garden of her own."

Steve seemed unbeatable. He had always had great cue action but now he had developed the 'killer instinct' and wanted to win everything. That first prize in 1981 was worth £20,000 out of a total of £75,000 prize money, and he must have earned a further £75,000 directly from tournaments. With Barry Hearn promoting him, Steve's earning capabilities were such that Hearn's prediction that Steve would become snooker's first millionnaire within a few years has already come true. The money Steve earns is wisely invested but he hasn't bought too much, other than a Porsche car, some nice chess men and a piano. Generally, his tastes haven't changed from the days when money was scarce.

It was almost unbelievable that Steve, having won every major title before he was twenty-five, should go through such a disappointing spell in the following twelve months. Apart from the 10-1 slamming from Tony Knowles—who was comparatively unknown—in his opening match in the 1982 world championships, Steve struggled in a year in which no one player completely dominated the snooker scene as he had done the previous year. The best Davis could do was to win the Langs Supreme in Scotland at the start of 1982, share the Hofmeister World Doubles title with Tony Meo, and win the Lada Classic and Pot Black for the first time.

The eclipse of Steve Davis in 1982 shocked his admirers and caused the cynics to ask whether the success of the Plumstead world-beater in 1981 was just a flash in the pan, but Steve and Barry Hearn did not panic. Since Ray Reardon's grip on the world title from 1973 to 1976 no defending champion had been able to retain the crown and no player had won it twice since the championships moved to the Crucible at Sheffield. Alex Higgins's second title showed a gap of ten years.

Steve's bad year taught him a lesson. He found that it was one thing becoming a world champion and quite another retaining the title. He found the pressure of taking part in exhibitions at £2,000 a time and his many business commitments hard to handle and he showed a loss of confidence as things began to go wrong for him. But Davis has too much talent to be pushed out of the top ratings and made up his mind to concentrate on getting back his old form which he did by sheer dedication.

He listened more than usually to the advice of his father and also put his game in the hands of Frank Callan, a Blackpool fishmonger, who had helped plot his first championship win. In 1983 he was back on form—winning important tournaments, looking an even better player than in 1981—and began as firm favourite to depose Alex Higgins, the 1982 champion. There simply was no stopping Davis and after he crushed Higgins in the semi-final the volatile Irishman was reduced to saying that when anybody comes up against Steve in that sort of form, he is unbeatable. So clinical was Steve's outlook that he simply laughed off a perhaps over-publicised death-threat and went on to crush Higgins 16-5 to put himself in the final against Cliff Thorburn. The match had to be halted for thirty-five minutes while the police scoured the Crucible Theatre with metal detectors and searched a thousand spectators.

The Hurricane tried a cocktail of lager and honey but it did nothing to help a 10-6 deficit from the afternoon session and the machine-like Davis just continued to eliminate him. And so to the final against an almost exhausted Thorburn. Once again it was a runaway victory for the unstoppable Davis who took the match 18-6 to become the first player to win the world title at the Crucible on two occasions. This time the crown was worth £30,000 to him and the successful year had earned him around £100,000, apart from the many perks outside the tournaments.

It was far from a great final because the result was a foregone conclusion from early on and only emphasised the ruthless efficiency of the young man from Plumstead, who showed no mercy to the tired Canadian. It was quite astonishing that the cool Steve should shed tears within minutes of becoming world champion for the second time. It is the sort of thing expected of Hurricane Higgins but not from the Ice Man of Snooker, but his mother Mrs Jean Davis revealed that she wasn't surprised and said, 'Beneath the ice-cool exterior at the table Steve is a very warm-hearted emotional person, full of fun and humour'. And, having got the emotion out of his system, Steve Davis was back to normal, went out with his dad for a few beers and was as relaxed as ever when playing an exhibition match a couple of days later.

Steve has a quiet, pleasing personality as well as a great deal of talent. He also has an astute adviser in Barry Hearn, a wealthy chartered accountant, who wasn't interested in snooker until he invested in the Luciana group of halls which included Romford in Essex

An unusual picture of Steve Davis at a Press Conference. What was the question that caused Steve so much thought?

where young Steve played. Hearn was so pleased with his first meeting with Davis that when he sold his halls in 1982, he retained Romford, spending a great deal of cash on improving what one day may have a plaque: 'Steve Davis played here!'

Whereas the middle-aged TV audience may never have approved wholeheartedly of the long-haired pop star image of some young players, Steve Davis was a different matter. Tall, red-haired and pale, he is clean-cut and always immaculately groomed. The former working-class boy who became an idol overnight now has a luxurious wardrobe and orders three pairs of trousers with each suit. Steve is also shrewd at weighing up the state of a rival's nerves. He admits that he too has occasionally been a victim of his own nerves. When very young he used to sweat during a game and would grab a towel and wipe his hands, but he decided it was too much of a give-away to the opposition so he now deliberately reaches for a towel every time he gets up to play and feels it is no longer a sign of pressure getting to him. What is remarkable is that Steve is always relaxed before games and drives himself many miles, sometimes at night, but always seems fresh when he starts to play in vital tournaments.

The question now to be asked is can Steve Davis, having got over his lapse of 1982, go on to win the world title as many times as Ray Reardon, John Pulman, Fred Davis or John Spencer? The days when a man like Joe Davis could dominate the championship for two decades have long gone and while Steve will not be easy to topple there are on the horizon a few hungry young men who will be trailing him in their bid to reach the top and become snooker millionaires. As the game's most eligible bachelor his fan mail from the ladies, both young and old, requires a staff to deal with. And many male fans are already beginning to ask if he will become even greater than Joe Davis. While I was, and still am, most impressed by this ice-cool clinical craftsman, it seems a little premature to compare a young man who has won the title twice with a man who had held the same crown for twenty years and then surrendered it while still at his peak.

With full supporting cast . . .

ONLY ten players have officially held the world snooker championship since it was instituted in 1927. I have already told you about the world-beaters. Joe Davis had no difficulty in holding off the small number of professionals and quit as champion in 1946. Fred Davis and John Pulman each won the title eight times in the restricted 1950s and 1960s. Ray Reardon was boss in the 1970s with six championships. John Spencer managed it three times, Walter Donaldson, Alex Higgins and Steve Davis twice each, while Terry Griffiths and Cliff Thorburn have been one-time champions. And Horace Lindrum's name is on the trophy for the 1952 event against McConachy when the rest of the professionals boycotted the championship.

Many other professionals have served their sport well and have come close to being world champions. Beaten finalists since the championships reverted to an open tournament in 1969 include Gary Owen, Warren Simpson, Eddie Charlton (twice), Graham Miles, Perrie Mans, Dennis Taylor and Doug Mountjoy. Players like Rex Williams and John Barrie put a tremendous amount into the game when it was needed, and this applies to David Taylor and John Virgo as well; and younger players like Tony Meo, Tony Knowles and Jimmy White with many exciting newcomers are breaking through from Junior Pot Black and the numerous tournaments now played.

It's nice to be the top dog, but for every winner there has to be a loser and one man who has contributed enormously to his sport in his native Australia and elsewhere is Eddie Charlton, an all-round sportsman who gave Ray Reardon two great fights before losing in the 1973 and 1975 finals. The second time it would be more correct to say the Aussie gave Ray a fright when, before eventually losing 31-30, Eddie led 29-23, slipped back to 29-30, and made it 30-30 before losing in the last frame, his biggest disappointment.

The enterprising Charlton actually promoted the 1975 championships in Australia. Billiards and snooker have always been big Down Under and while it is accepted that Walter Lindrum was the best billiards player in the world, Australians of different generations will argue whether Horace Lindrum or Eddie Charlton was their finest snooker champion.

Eddie is one of the most enterprising sportsmen I've met. Brought up at Swansea, a mining and fishing town some hundred miles from Sydney, he not only showed early promise at snooker as a ten-year-old in his grandfather's saloon, and made his first century break before he was fifteen, but was outstanding at soccer, swimming, surfing, cricket, running and boxing and was a proud carrier of the Olympic torch at Melbourne in 1956. He won three amateur boxing titles and three amateur New South Wales snooker championships before turning professional in 1963, and has won the Australian professional title every year except 1968. He had three Pot Black wins in Britain but has not won a major title here: he reckons conditions, tables and lighting are superior in Australia and is willing to back himself heavily against any player in the world in his own country.

It was due to Eddie's success in Pot Black that the Australian Broadcasting Commission decided to buy the series, and later a similar tournament known as the Winfield Masters, featuring eight top professionals, started in Australia and now has a television audience of millions. I have been making annual trips Down Under to commentate on this tournament and have much respect for Eddie. Though in his early fifties, his energy is remarkable. No matter what hour of the day or night I arrive in Sydney, I know Eddie will be there to meet me. He is a real showman and an astute businessman; years ago he had the idea of taking Eddie Charlton through the length and breadth of his huge country with his own large truck carrying a full-size table, scoreboard and all equipment plus seating for five hundred.

Eddie is one of the most solid players in the game. His style reminds me of Walter Donaldson for he is also a straight ball player. And nobody produces more sensational trick shots. Once in Hobart we thought he was joking when he asked an attractive Winfield

The line-up for the Australian Winfield Masters in 1982 included four world champions: left to right, Ted Lowe, Alex Higgins, Steve Davis, Eddie Charlton, John Spencer, Ray Reardon, Ian Anderson, Tony Meo and famous Australian referee Ron Tscherne.

hostess if she would help him with a trick shot by lying on the table with a piece of chalk between her teeth with the blue ball resting on it. The girl also thought Eddie was joking but when he assured her he was serious and that no harm would come, she sportingly agreed. He then set the cue ball on two pieces of chalk on top of the cushion, played it on to the blue ball and knocked it from her mouth down the table into the top pocket! But now several British professionals are doing the same trick.

His failure to capture the world title is the one frustration of his life. He could still do it but realises that the task gets more difficult every year as the competition gets tougher and younger.

WHEN Leicester Square Hall re-opened in 1946 there were only five established professionals: Joe and Fred Davis, Sidney Smith, Horace Lindrum and Walter Donaldson. When Joe decided to retire I began searching for youngsters and was encouraged by the form of John Pulman and John Barrie. Often among the spectators during their Leicester Square days was a keen teenager, always accompanied by his father, a successful Midlands businessman. Rex Williams was brought to London by his dad especially to take lessons from Joe Davis and on all the trips they took in a session at Leicester Square. This went on

Eddie Charlton is interviewed by Ted Lowe while demonstrating trick shots during the Winfield Tournament.

for a few years and little did I realise that four years after our opening night Rex Williams would be making his debut on the famous table in a 71-frame match against John Pulman.

Born in 1934, Rex was encouraged at billiards and snooker by his father from the age of thirteen. He won the Boys championships at both games and at seventeen, in 1951, was the youngest All-England amateur champion. Yet another seventeen years passed before he claimed the world's professional billiards championship when he travelled to New Zealand and beat Clark McConachy, who was seventy-three and hadn't defended that title since 1951. Rex's first love was billiards but he was good at the twenty-two ball game, as he proved when twice challenging John Pulman for the world crown. He is proud to be the second player officially to equal Joe Davis's 147 break, which he achieved against Mannie Francisco in South Africa in 1965. After his father died Rex moved into the business world and has become one of the game's ambassadors and a respected administrator as chairman of the Professional Players Association. Rex resigned in anger when a £500 fine was placed on him but the trouble was sorted out and he remains chairman. His voice has also become familiar to millions as a member of the BBC's commentary team.

John Barrie was another young man who helped to boost the game in the immediate post-war years. Remarkably, he was born with his heart on the right side—(or wrong side!)—of his body. Though a good snooker player, like Rex, he excelled at billiards. I had some enjoyable times in John's company. He lacked the 'killer' touch, which was probably the reason he didn't win a world title, but was great fun and we had many laughs in that tiny office of mine at Leicester Square which was also used as a changing room. John was always a gentleman but very untidy and usually when getting into a dinner suit, would leave his vest or pants or an odd sock lying around. Whenever Syd Lee, a tremendous player in his day and practical joker, dropped into my room he would take delight in picking up one of the odd garments and either hiding it or sometimes even throwing it out of the window. There were great laughs when later Barrie would be changing back into his normal suit and couldn't find sock, tie or shirt! The room was three flights up and I am sure that when eventually that part of the building was pulled down the workmen discovered many old garments belonging to Barrie Smith.

Barrie is one of the professionals who got away. His family had always been comfortable and his father ran a thriving tobacconist's business and a hotel at Wisbech in Cambridgeshire. Barrie and his wife Joan took over the White Lion Hotel in the town; I still have fun when I go there and we indulge in a little nostalgia. He didn't reach the very pinnacle but had a tremendous influence on the game.

Perrie Mans is South Africa's most consistent player. He hails from a snooker family, and he and his wife Hester have four children. His father, the South African champion before him, had beaten Joe Davis at Thurston's when receiving one black. His brother Piet, also a promising player, had his career cut short through a mining accident. His sister Minnie was also highly rated. Perrie, a left-hander, has never won the world title but has been a giant-killer. He knocked out John Spencer to reach the quarter-final in 1974. Two years later he

Perrie Mans.

beat Graham Miles and Jimmy Meadowcroft to make the semi-finals, and in 1978 became the first South African to play in the final, knocking out John Spencer, Graham Miles and Fred Davis before going down to Ray Reardon. His most successful performance was to win the Benson and Hedges Masters in 1979 with wins over Cliff Thorburn, Ray Reardon and Alex Higgins. He impressed me when winning pot Black at his first attempt in 1977, his better period.

Though the game has not advanced in South Africa as it has done in Canada, Perrie, an insurance agent, travels his country encouraging youngsters. He is a hero there. After winning the South African amateur title in 1960 he took the professional crown from Freddie van Rensburg at his first attempt in 1965 and kept it until losing to Derek Mienie fourteen years later, winning it back again in 1980.

Perrie, who gained the nick-name of Billy the Thud, remains the boss in the Transvaal. His only real challenger is Silvino Francisco, who was born in Capetown of Portuguese origin and has made a 147 break. Like most South African pros, Silvino had trouble raising the cash to come to Britain, but did so in 1982 and the trip was worthwhile because he reached the quarter-finals of the world championships. Other players encouraged by Mans' progress include Jimmy van Rensburg, Derek Mienie and Roy Amdor.

Another top player and personality yet to become world champion is Doug Mountjoy, twice Welsh amateur champion and also world amateur champion in 1968 and 1976, who looked like setting the professional circuit alight when he turned professional, collecting the Benson and Hedges Masters in 1977, the U.K. championship the next year and many other tournaments.

I first met the quiet Welshman at Prestatyn in 1974 when my old friend Sir Fred Pontin asked me to devise a snooker tournament that might add a couple of weeks' bookings on to his holiday camps. Over a coffee and brandy the Pontins Snooker Festival was born. I worked it out with an Open tournament so that all entries would be reduced to twenty-four players who would compete over one week. In addition, I suggested eight top professionals to play in a separate professional tournament as entertainment for the holidaymakers. Then the eight pros would join in against the twenty-four survivors who would receive handicaps to find the Open champion. There was a £1,000 prize for the Open winner and also a £1,000 for the professional visitor.

I was delighted with a first entry of just under 400. Doug Mountjoy was the Welsh

Sir Fred Pontin has a few words to say over the mike during one of the Pontins Snooker Festivals at Prestatyn camp.

amateur champion at the time, but was almost unknown outside Wales. He soon altered this situation by taking the £1,000 prize. Receiving 25 points he beat Ray Reardon, then world champion, 7-4. As a professional in 1979 he went back to Prestatyn and won the professional final, beating Graham Miles, which made him the only player to win the Pontins professional and Open finals—and he won the amateur event twice.

When Doug became a pro, he was invited to compete in Pot Black 1977 and finished runner-up; he won the event next year and made 101 for the highest break, and finished runner-up in 1979, again scoring the highest break.

Doug Mountjoy and wife Yvonne celebrate another victory.

Doug was born at Tir-y-berth in Glamorgan and played the game for fun as a boy. On leaving school he followed his father into the pits and soon became Welsh junior champion. At twenty-six, he took the Welsh amateur in 1968 and again in 1974 and won the world amateur crown in Johannesburg in 1976 having already held it in 1968. He has a pleasing personality and quiet sense of fun. The only thing about him that is out of character with the Welsh is that Doug can't sing! I think he is the first Welshman I have ever met who can't. I made this discovery on a trip to Australia in 1980. After the hard work was finished at Sydney we went on to Brisbane and at the end of play, our hosts took us out for a tremendous seafood dinner. As the wine flowed the party developed and everybody had to do an act or tell a story. As Doug was Welsh, our hosts insisted he should render 'We'll keep a welcome in the hillsides!' To do justice to Mountjoy, he did everything to resist but we twisted his arm and he obliged with support from Eddie Charlton and Ray Reardon. I know Doug won't mind me saying he brought the house down, though 'A welcome in the Vales' sounded more like 'Dingos in the Dales'. But Doug was a splendid sport and everybody had a grand evening. He was assured by our hosts that there would always be a welcome for him in Australia, as well as in Wales.

Mountjoy is dedicated to the game and practises for hours on the table at his home, and though a settled family man with his wife Yvonne, daughter Yvette and son Andrew, he will travel anywhere to give an exhibition and seems to have little interest in the business world. Since turning pro he has won most major tournaments and though the world title escaped him when Steve Davis beat him in 1981, he had the consolation not only of reaching the final and collecting £10,000 but of setting up a new championship record break of 145 when beating Ray Reardon in the semi-final. That break was worth £5,000. I was lucky enough to be the commentator for that memorable frame that thrilled millions. Of course, Cliff Thorburn then set up a new championship record with 147 in 1983.

John Virgo has beaten the best players in the world without winning the supreme title. This is probably due to the fact that despite his brilliance when in top form, consistency is not his strongest asset and at times a volatile temperament frustrates his ambitions.

Born at Rochdale, the birthplace of Gracie Fields, John is among the most entertaining players on the circuit. He has the humour that makes folk from Lancashire good comedians and is a top mimic, mostly at the expense of his fellow professionals. As for trick shots, there are few better entertainers. John won the Boys championship at fifteen, the Junior title at eighteen and was Youths champion at twenty-two; he also played in many successful internationals for England between 1970 and 1976 when he turned professional. Following his early successes, he expected to make a bigger impression on the senior world of snooker but it didn't work out that way and for three years, until he was thirty, he hesitated to turn professional. Perhaps a little cocky as a youth, his ego was tamed in 1975 when facing Ray Reardon, then world champion, in the Pontins Festival Open final—John received 25 points and was whacked 7-1. He was about to turn professional but was so shattered by the result, believing that no player in the world could give him 25 start *and* a drumming, that he delayed for another year and it was three more years before he won his first major tournament at thirty-three, when he took the Coral U.K. crown and his biggest pay-packet of £4,500, beating world champion Terry Griffiths in the final.

It was a controversial final. Virgo led 11-7 but was penalised two frames after turning up late due to a misunderstanding of the time of play. John was sitting in his hotel in Preston when he should have been in the Guildhall. The penalty not only annoyed Virgo but seemed to disturb Griffiths. Both players missed shots they would normally sink. The score went to 12-12 and Griffiths went ahead but John produced some of his best snooker to make it all square and then slammed the world champion 78-16 to win 14-13. His best per-

John Virgo crowns himself after winning the Coral U.K. championship in 1979. John is one of snooker's characters and an expert in the art of mimicry.

formance in the world championships was a losing semi-final to Dennis Taylor a few months before his U.K. triumph.

Virgo was regarded as a big-head in his early days and often misunderstood. He is honestly blunt and sometimes makes himself unpopular by speaking his mind; he admits he can't switch on and off to suit everybody. He can't talk to opponents without losing some concentration and some opponents consequently regard him as churlish, but he says he can't help that interpretation because he plays to win. 'You get nothing for losing, do you?' he asks. In fact, his TV image of a grim, bearded performer does little justice to his true character. John can be so funny, especially when relaxing over a few drinks, and I have evidence he has a heart of gold. One day I went racing at Newmarket, picked a few winners and met so many friends that the champagne flowed too freely and it all continued back at the Newmarket Moat House Hotel. Next morning I felt fragile at the breakfast table, attempting to face a plate of bacon and eggs. The colour of my face must have told a story. And John Virgo, whom I hadn't noticed in the dining room, came across with a packet of Alka-Seltzer, a large glass of water and a pot of black coffee. That friendly act put me back in the land of the living. An hour later he produced a bottle of champagne for his racing friends and myself. I wished him a successful day at his favourite pastime.

Graham Miles, from Birmingham, could be used to illustrate that old saying that nice guys finish second. Though he played as a boy he was twenty-two before making his first century break. He won the Midlands Amateur title but when he turned professional in 1969 at the age of twenty-eight, he did not win any major tournaments, though he did register a 147 break. His best performance was reaching the quarter-final of the world championships in 1973. I included him as a reserve for Pot Black 1974 and luck was with him. Fred Davis went sick and Graham stepped in, won the tournament and recorded the highest break. His final win against John Spencer brought him instant TV fame and an uplift in his game and he shone in the 1974 world championships, reaching the final,

Australia bound. Ted Lowe shares a joke with Graham Miles and John Spencer on the 'plane.

although he was then rather outclassed by Ray Reardon 22-12. Graham kept on a winning note by taking Pot Black a second year running but was thwarted from a third win when well beaten by Doug Mountjoy in 1978. His 'always the bridesmaid but never the bride' record also applied in the 1976 Benson and Hedges Masters when after taking care of Higgins and Spencer he lost to Reardon in the final although he won the Australian Masters in 1976. He didn't reach another major tournament final for three years, when he was beaten by Spencer. So disappointed was he with his own form after its early promise that Graham contemplated quitting, but persevered and had some reward when he took the Tolly Cobbold Classic, thrashing Cliff Thorburn 5-1.

Miles had first caught my eye with his unorthodox style. His cue virtually rested under his ear. Yet he could build breaks from nowhere with a gentle approach that made bolder potters fear him. When his form began to go wrong he understandably lost confidence, switching cues and even resorting to the Canadian two-piece which he soon abandoned in favour of one of his old cues. Eventually he changed his action, lifting his head so that the cue now rested almost under his chin. This improved his sighting. Miles, now in his early forties, may not now join the world champions but still loves the game and will keep at it for fun when his tournament days are over. He owns a very successful club.

When Dennis Taylor was only ten, he spent hours watching his father and older brother Martin playing at Coalisland, Co. Tyrone, where he was born. By the time he was fourteen he could beat them both. He was then only earning £4 a week as a labourer so at seventeen decided to cross the Irish Sea in search of a better job and join an aunt living at Darwen, Lancashire. Though working long hours in a paper mill, he found time to play snooker and won the East Lancashire senior title when eighteen. At twenty-one he was chosen by England (as a resident) in an amateur international against Wales. He turned professional at twenty-three and in 1974 played brilliantly to reach the Canadian Open final. His best world championship feats took him into the 1975 and 1977 semi-finals and in 1979 he eliminated Steve Davis and put defending champion Ray Reardon and John Virgo out before going down in the final against Terry Griffiths.

Dennis is typically Irish when it comes to a gamble. He had taken a job as manager of the Elite Club at Accrington to give himself more practice. In 1974 with only £200 saved and a wife and two children to support, Dennis, now twenty-four and living at Blackburn, quit his job at the Elite and decided to have a go in the John Player international at Toronto. He knew he would need at least to reach the final to break even financially, and achieved this target, beating Alex Higgins in the semi-final before losing to Cliff Thorburn in the final.

He was the youngest player to be invited to Pot Black 1975 and he finished runner-up. In the same year he went to Australia for the world championships and beat Perrie Mans, Fred Davis and Gary Owen before losing to Eddie Charlton in the semi-final. He also reached the world semi-final in 1977, going down to Thorburn. In 1976 he finished runner-up again in Pot Black. He got immense satisfaction from winning the Irish professional title by

Dennis Taylor introduces his new 'headlamp' spectacles in February 1983.

beating Higgins 21-15 for his first major prize and retained it by beating Patsy Fagan the following year. Dennis has developed a very pleasing personality and is a great teller of stories. He could stand up with many of today's comedians, which adds to his popularity whenever he appears. Dennis is one of those popular players who is always among the top names.

David Taylor, unrelated to Dennis, is known as the Silver Fox—a name I gave him in commentary. A Manchester hairdresser, he won the English world amateur championships in 1968 and turned professional, but he made little impression in the tournaments and only just about made a living with exhibitions. It took him ten years to get into the big time and

David Taylor, the Silver Fox.

that was in the 1978 U.K. Championships, when he recorded handsome wins over Patsy Fagan, John Virgo and Alex Higgins before losing to Doug Mountjoy in the final. His most merited break performance was a consecutive 130, 140 and 139, a world record, at Butlin's Holiday Camp at Minehead in Somerset. His best world championship effort was in 1980 when he beat Ray Edmonds, Fred Davis and Ray Reardon to reach the semi-final before going down to Cliff Thorburn, who went on to win the title. In 1981 he finished runner-up to the all-conquering Steve Davis in the Yamaha Organs Trophy final and collected £5,000. In 1982 the Manchester player reached only his third big money final and once more was frustrated in his attempt to win his first major tournament when beaten by Tony Knowles.

He lived up to his Silver Fox title with cunning safety play but Tony, making his own first major championship breakthrough, finished too strongly. David had the consolation of his biggest ever prize of £10,000 but having made a 101 break in the second round, saw the £1,200 highest break prize snatched from him by Knowles, who came up with 144 in the ninth frame in the final session.

David is a self-contained loner who neither smokes nor drinks, and mainly avoids the social side of snooker. He still resides in Manchester.

Tony Knowles, an art student from Bolton, abandoned a career as a graphic artist to become a snooker champion after staying on for higher education until eighteen. He was not accepted as a professional until he was twenty-five and another two years passed before he became an overnight star by thrashing Steve Davis 10-1 in the opening round of Steve's first defence of the world crown in 1982. After his triumph in 1981, Steve had swept all before him in the big tournaments. He had been cracked up as invincible when he crashed to then little-known Knowles. Tony did not go on to win the world title but his success inspired him and a few months later he won his first major championship at twenty-seven, taking the Jameson Open and first prize of £22,000 plus £1,200 for the highest break.

Knowles, an intelligent young man, had always argued that promoters, sponsors and

Tony Knowles (right) discusses a point from his semi-final match with Cliff Thorburn in the 1983 Embassy World Championship.

television should encourage lesser names rather than concentrate on the stars. Now seen on TV annihilating Davis, he had joined the elite. A tall, dark and handsome bachelor, he became the target of hundreds of young ladies and his 'phone hardly stopped as he was openly asked for dates. After the Jameson victory he received around 4,000 letters and one girl he had not even met sent her father's private jet and flew him to her home. Another female admirer booked a candlelit dinner and sent a car to pick him up. Another sent him a rose every day during one tournament.

Such a value is set on snooker-stars today that Tony has had his hands insured for £500,000. I hope Knowles doesn't allow this sort of heady life to interfere with his future. He seems a sensible young man but look how Steve Davis flopped a year after his wonderful run of success. This wasn't due to being chased by young ladies, but that Steve was taking part in so many exhibitions and sometimes three shows a day that he seemed jaded when the 1982 championships began. The bookmakers listed him as 5-2 favourite which was made a nonsense by the way he played against Knowles. He was so edgy before the match began that he ordered photographers to leave.

Despite breaking through as a personality, Knowles was soon to realise how competitive modern snooker is when early in 1983 he was whitewashed 5-0 by Kirk Stevens in the £65,000 Lada Classic at Warrington. Tony was powerless as Kirk rattled up three 60-odd breaks and the result made the Bolton player appear an also-ran. But that defeat could be the best thing that has happened to him in his great drive to become a world champion. It's not only tough at the top—it's tough even getting there, as he discovered when missing an easy pink against Thorburn for a place in the 1983 final.

Jimmy White is the youngest of the established professionals and the most exciting character since Alex Higgins first crashed the headlines in the early 1970s. White, a Cockney lad, has some of the strengths and the weaknesses of the Hurricane but, after getting himself some bad publicity as a teenager, has quietened down and though his play has been more subdued he has shown more responsibility and has years ahead of him to attempt to join the world champions.

Jimmy was a pupil at the Ernest Bevin School at Tooting and is the first to admit he is no great academic, but he is forever grateful to a most understanding Headmaster, Mr Beattie, who realised that Jimmy's natural gift at snooker would serve him better in life than any attempt to turn him into a learned scholar. So instead of lecturing Master White on the evils of attending a billiards hall when so young, Mr Beattie made a Solomon-like decision and gave Jimmy permission to play snooker in the afternoons. With this official approval the boy chalked up his first century at thirteen and could already beat most men in the local hall; soon he had developed into the most precocious snooker player we have known. He was British boys' champion at fifteen, youngest English amateur champion at sixteen and youngest world amateur title holder at eighteen.

White showed what we might expect from him when he reached the final of the Pontins Open; though well beaten by Steve Davis who conceded 30 points, Jimmy was not discouraged. Given the opportunity to play an exhibition against world champion Reardon, and receiving 21 points, he was given a lesson in the finer arts of the game but came up with a 116 break which had Ray applauding him and forecasting a bright future. He showed the same gift for producing the big break on the big occasion when winning the English Amateur title, beating Northern champion Dave Martin at Helston, Cornwall. He knocked up 130, smashing the championship record, though the B.S.C.C. did not accept it since they were not satisfied with the two top pockets. He was a member of the London team at sixteen and played for England at seventeen, but a lack of self-discipline got him into trouble which threatened his future career when only eighteen.

Playing for England against Wales at Pontins, Jimmy let his hair down and had a few drinks, a very easy thing for a teenager to do at a holiday camp. He played poorly in his last match, to be beaten by Stan Newbury which meant the championship went to Wales. The England party felt White had let them down. Some officials were so furious with Jimmy's somewhat irresponsible behaviour that they decided to punish him. He was told that the

Jimmy White.

committee had decided not to send him to Tasmania to bid for the world amateur championship. Jimmy was not only chastened but heart-broken. He accepted that he had asked for a ticking off, but had never thought anything like that would happen. Luckily, he had a few friends in high places who felt the punishment was too severe for the crime. Following an outcry the ruling body was put under so much pressure that they met again and while confirming that they thought he had let the side down and reprimanding him, they allowed him to make the trip to Tasmania. He more than justified their mercy, becoming at eighteen the youngest player to win the world amateur crown, overwhelming the Australian Ron Atkin 11-2. On the way home he won the Indian championship at Calcutta. His performance allowed him to set up another record and he was accepted as the youngest professional. Making his debut in the 1981 world championships as the youngest-ever competitor, he won his two qualifying matches before coming up against an on-form Steve Davis in the first round, but put up a tremendous fight before losing 10-8. Davis went on to win the title.

Once in the big league, Jimmy realised he was still a boy playing among men; he was not able to sweep all before him as he thought he might and on one or two occasions he had to learn the hard way against champions like Steve Davis and Ray Reardon. So Jimmy has learned how to behave. He is now a married man and through his manager Geoff Lomas is attempting to retrieve those lost school lessons. He is still young and the talent is there.

Tony Meo hails from Tooting and went a little earlier to the same school as Jimmy White. Born of Italian parents who settled in London, Tony had some of White's youthful flair and made a 147 break at the Pot Black Centre at Clapham in 1977 when only seventeen. Though not officially recognised, he was still an amateur and the youngest player to make a maximum break.

The Tooting snooker connoisseurs spotted him as something special when only twelve; by the time he was seventeen he had won several amateur championships and he became Junior champion at eighteen. He was determined to turn professional. Steve Davis, a couple of years his senior, was also contemplating joining the circuit when they met in the Pontins Open final in 1978 and Tony impressed Ray Reardon and John Spencer, who had competed in the professional final, when he lost to Davis by only 7-6. He was accepted as a pro at nineteen. He didn't win any tournaments but eliminated some of the top stars including Steve Davis, Doug Mountjoy and David Taylor, and in his first world championships in 1980 put out Jimmy van Rensburg in the qualifying round and took Alex Higgins to 10-9 in the first round. Next year he again won his qualifying games and beat John Virgo in the first round but was disappointed in 1982, losing to Perrie Mans in the first round.

One of Meo's best victories was when overwhelming Alex Higgins 6-1 in the 1981 Lucania Professional championship final. He showed his versatility soon after when I called upon him as a late substitute for the Winfield Masters in Sydney and he beat Cliff Thorburn and John Spencer to win the event in his first visit to Australia.

For me, Tony's best performance was when partnering Steve Davis in the Hofmeister

Tony Meo takes the stage at the Crucible Theatre, Sheffield.

World Doubles championships at the Crystal Palace late in 1982. Steve and Tony built up an overnight lead of 10-2 against Terry Griffiths and Doug Mountjoy and next day polished off the three frames required for victory. It was Tony, and not Steve, who was responsible for the crushing of Griffiths and Mountjoy with devastating attacking play throughout the week and especially in the final. But the early finish left the sponsors and ITV crew in something of a dilemma. The customers had paid £9 for the night session, the players were not too happy with the Crystal Palace, complaining that the large hall was none too warm, and there were also many empty seats. So to try and help the fans and TV, all four players agreed to play a £1,000 singles charity series to satisfy disappointed spectators.

Tony had been playing professionally for four years without winning a major tournament, although in 1983 he had wins against Jimmy White and Doug Mountjoy. But the Hofmeister World Doubles saw his finest hour to date. Not only were Griffiths and Mountjoy embarrassed by their lack of action in the final but a happier Steve Davis was also a comparative onlooker as Tooting Tony sunk ball after ball and knocked up a 124 break in the process. With Steve he shared the £24,000 prize plus £2,000 for that highest break. The championship form had been a long time coming but Tony agreed it was all well worth waiting for. He and Terry Griffiths have joined the Barry Hearn stable.

CHAPTER 6

Trouble in Paradise

I HAVE thoroughly enjoyed putting on record my forty years in top-class snooker. I have seen the game develop and flourish beyond my wildest dreams and as we approach the 1984 world championships, snooker, thanks to television, has one of the biggest viewing audiences in sport with an average of seventeen million watching the world championships over recent years. From the original four competitors in these championships there were a record seventy-four competing at the Crucible in 1983 and, no doubt, numbers will continue to increase. From the £6.10s. Joe Davis received as the first world champion, the value of the crown had increased to £30,000 when young Steve Davis collected his second title, while runner-up Cliff Thorburn picked up £28,000 made up of £15,000 prize money plus £10,000 for making the maximum break with yet another £3,000 for the highest break in the championships.

There are more and more goodies to come. Embassy have poured fortunes into these championships and plan to invest still more in sponsorship. The mind almost boggles when I realise that the professional snooker players, once the Cinderella Men of sport, will share £180,000 in prizes for the Embassy event in 1984 and £280,000 in 1985. There are many young men in the wings dreaming of joining the likes of Steve Davis as one of the most privileged performers in sport. So from the once struggling players in smoky backrooms and tatty clubs, the world of professional snooker in the 1980s has become a sporting paradise—a land of milk, honey and gold.

Yet I must end my story with a warning that unless players and their managers make a common-sense appraisal of the future of the game, paradise could be lost forever. There is already trouble in paradise caused by sheer greed—though I don't blame the young snooker players any more than I do the young stars of soccer, tennis, golf and other sports, because we live in an age in which money and worldly possessions are in more demand than at any other period and, as human nature doesn't change, I suppose you cannot blame the stars chasing and grabbing for more and more. Sadly, an insatiable appetite is never satisfied, but I wonder how long snooker will maintain its astonishing popularity among so many millions if the present stars persist with their financial demands. There is a grave danger that they are about to throttle the golden goose and, while the present crop of champions can

Steve Davis's first entry into big business was to sign a contract for cues with Riley Billiards immediately after winning the Coral U.K. professional championship in 1979. Steve signs for Riley director Bruce Donkin.

philosophise that Jack is all right, the boom years of snooker will fade away if millions of television viewers begin to switch off.

There is no doubt already that while the young players are richer than ever they are not as relaxed or happy as the old players who struggled to pay the rent. The fun has gone out of the game since it has been taken over by big business though to be fair to the stars of to-day, they are nearly all financially guided by managers. I am certain this is true; though I concede that in my autumn years I see the game in a different light compared with the late 1940s and 1950s.

I have told you of the fun we had at Leicester Square Hall in the days when money was so short that I and several of the professionals couldn't afford a car or even a taxi to take us home late at night. Yet those hungry players of yesterday projected a dignified image both on and away from the table and were always ready to find time to help the game. In the 1980s nobody seems to approach anybody else without the catch-phrase response: 'How much?' I recall only last season a leading and respected star refusing to offer one of his cues to a charity auction because the £500 fee for a two-frames exhibition was in his words 'a mere pittance'. He arrived at the show without his own cue to give the exhibition. There was a time when a snooker pro considered himself to be a real trouper and it was unheard of for a player to miss a show. Today we all too often hear of a capacity audience kept waiting and indeed a show sometimes cancelled because of a non-appearance of the 'star'. When this happens it is disgraceful. Surely, they have to give as well as take from the game.

For years it was accepted that BBC's Pot Black was the one show that brought fame and fortune to many of today's big names. Yet on more than one occasion this tournament that rescued snooker from bankruptcy has been in jeopardy because of money. The stars have short memories. Several players want it sponsored and I leave it to the readers' imagination what sort of prize money the stars are looking for. Why should the BBC sell their copyright of such a successful snooker event on TV?

The world championships, with the tremendous financial backing from Embassy, have become the biggest outside broadcast in sport, even outstripping Wimbledon tennis fortnight. The snooker championships go on for seventeen days and are played morning, afternoon and evenings and on Sundays. The games take place, come rain or shine. This means the event can be seen on the screen from 10.30am till perhaps 2am next day and in the case of one Thorburn match in 1983, until nearly 4am! Consider the growth of TV coverage. In 1976 snooker was seen on Grandstand for only 42 minutes plus Pot Black during the whole year. The 1983 championships alone provided 90 hours viewing.

Yet while the prize money and TV coverage grows, I still warn the professionals and their managers to take heed about the future of the game. Not only has the fun gone out of the game but money has become so important that the pressure on the players is becoming unbearable. The 1983 championships produced more crises among the stars than any I have witnessed in forty years. The tension produced one of the dullest finals with only 10 million watching Steve Davis's runaway victory over Cliff Thorburn compared with 15 million witnessing the emotional win of Alex Higgins over Ray Reardon in 1982 and 17 million when Steve Davis won the title for the first time in 1981.

Surely the reason for Thorburn's poor challenge to Steve, who was in tremendous form, was exhaustion from seventeen days of tension. Cliff developed a slower game and in 1983 television viewers saw him playing until 4am against Terry Griffiths and also in the early hours of the morning against Kirk Stevens. He was lifted by his 147 maximum break but then depressed by the bad news that back in Canada his wife had lost their second child which she was carrying. Cliff seemed to age in those seventeen days with the worry and strain of his late matches. He looked worn out before he began the final against Davis. He had earned £10,000 for the 147 pus £3,000 for the highest break. Had he won his second championship, he would have received a total of £43,000. But is it worth it?

With Steve also playing slower snooker and determined to recapture his 1981 form when he swept all before him, there was never any chance of this final approaching the excitement of the Higgins-Reardon match and there was complete anti-climax when the dedicated and ruthless Steve took charge from the opening session. It was the least entertaining final I have had to commentate on. So though Embassy increased their prize money from £15,300 for their first sponsorship in 1976 to £135,000 in 1983, and it will be up to £280,000 in 1985, there is still a grave danger of the TV audience decreasing if the viewers are not sufficiently entertained. If professionals continue to drag the game into the early hours of the morning or drop out of committed engagements to pick up fatter fees, the world championships as we know them today will be hard pressed to survive in the 1990s.

Not only did Cliff Thorburn end up physically shattered, but 1983 saw other stars needing medical attention, some of it from sheer nerves and stress. Kirk Stevens had to see a doctor because of a touch of glandular fever. Jimmy White, after being well beaten by Tony Meo, rushed from the table because he had built up so much tension that he was emotionally upset. Tony Knowles developed a slight rash before facing Thorburn in the semi-final and had to leave the session once, and was so nervous that he missed comparatively easy shots he would normally have taken in his stride: missing a simple pink prevented him reaching his first world final. Alex Higgins, the defending world champion, was also a victim of nerves with a stomach upset before going out to face Steve Davis in 1983 semi-final. It just goes to show that the vast amount of cash at stake takes its toll on the players who are so much richer, but far less relaxed, than the happy-go-lucky professionals of the past.

Now I am talking, as we all do as the years roll on, about the good old days. Perhaps they weren't so good when footballers had a maximum wage of £20 a week and the fans who supported them earned far less. Yet England had a great soccer side and there was no fan violence. Tennis players such as Rod Laver dominated Wimbledon without displays of bad temper and bad language. When our cricketers won back the Ashes from Australia they let their hair down and champagne flowed freely but the cricketers and the spectators behaved with dignity. Whether or not you agree with me, I assure you that ugly manners, bad language and bad sportsmanship was a rarity in Britain in the 1950s. Sport was then sport and had not been taken over by the money-minded moguls who set out to turn young athletes into tycoons and themselves into super-tycoons.

So far snooker has not descended to the level of some sports which have become almost obscene, but the dangers are there as the tendency to avarice takes over. More players are disputing referee's decisions. More players are forgetting that they owe something to the game that has made them rich. It's like inflation. Unless a positive effort is made to retain snooker basically as a sport and not just a money-grabbing exercise, the boom of the 1970s and 1980s could end. If millions of TV fans switch off so, too, will the sponsors. And paradise will be lost to the players through greed.

You see, I entered the world of top professional snooker in 1945 when the big occasion was that epic world championship final between Joe Davis and Horace Lindrum and I was

Bill Werbeniuk shares a pint with Dennis Taylor after winning the Winfield Masters in Auckland, New Zealand, in July 1983—the last snooker tournament of the 1982/3 season.

soon to open that famous home of the game, Leicester Square Hall. There were few stars but the few performed immaculately both on and away from the billiards table. Snooker was their business and the stars were professionals at that business in every sense. They appreciated their financial rewards which, without being high, were comfortable, but it involved hard work touring the clubs playing matches or giving exhibitions because there were no big tournaments on television and only small sponsorship. The average income was between £50 and £100 per week and to be sure of maintaining this wage they always had to command the respect of the public. Today there is a cluster of stars, the snooker calendar is one continuous run of sponsored tournaments and the prizes are astronomic. Sadly, many clubs are unable to pay the high fees demanded. I don't begrudge the young players today's earnings but even the greatest of them must realise that snooker is greater than any individual player.

Last summer I returned from my seventh trip to Australia and my first to New Zealand, each visit being to cover a big tournament for their television networks. 1983 saw the Canadians dominate. Cliff Thorburn, fully recovered from the exhausting world championships at Sheffield, took all honours in the $100,000 tournament with its $20,000 first prize and $2,000 for the highest break, while Bill Werbeniuk repeated a Canadian triumph in Auckland, winning $11,000 from the $30,000 prize money. But some British stars didn't take it quite so seriously. Tony Knowles, making his first visit to Australia decided on a night out before the semi-final and lost 5-0. I hope the heavy defeat taught Tony something. And in Sydney Alex Higgins failed to attend both the Sponsors' Press reception and the Final presentation. In New Zealand the complex Irishman upset the Press and made some ill-timed remarks in a TV interview. Naturally, the sponsors were displeased with Alex's lack of courtesy and whether you like or dislike some reporters, there wouldn't be any sponsors if the media showed no interest in the game. Life is all about give and take. I left Australia wondering whether the Irishman would receive another invitation.

As I end my story, snooker is getting even bigger and the prizes in 1984 and 1985 will continue to increase. The bonanza brought about by television and by Pot Black in particular is growing all the time, world-wide. I only hope the players don't allow greed to prick their lucrative balloon, for I take pride in playing a part in making it all possible.

Index of Personalities

(entries in italics indicate appearances in photographs)